GOOD
MAN

"We modern men are facing our biggest identity crisis in centuries. Nathan Clarkson's *Good Man* offers a wholistic and biblical lens through which to view our lives as sons of the King. In a world obsessed with noise, fame, and greatness, we have the opportunity to live quiet, courageous, epic lives filled with authentic goodness. Christ Himself beckons: The time is short. The stakes are high. Adventure awaits."

Jared Brock, author of *Bearded Gospel Men*
and *A Year of Living Prayerfully*

"In a culture that is overwhelmed with increasing male suicide rates, more and more mass shootings committed by men, and continued male abuses, we are in desperate need of a fresh and real hope for today's culture of men. In *Good Man*, Nathan does an exquisite job of taking us on a journey that redefines what it means to be a good, not a perfect, man. I pray this book will make it into the hands of as many hurting men as possible."

Kait Warman, relationship expert, speaker,
and founder of Heart of Dating

"Nathan Clarkson's newest book, *Good Man*, is an intimate and honest portrayal of what God considers to be a good man. Nathan strips away our preconceived notions and then brilliantly and biblically empowers us to feel whole, hopeful, and inspired—the very things that God desires men to embody in their everyday lives! It's a must-read!"

Guy Lia, cowriter of *Marriage Triggers*,
TV and film producer, and founder of The Firepit

"*Good Man* takes a unique dive into mental health and society today. Being a guy in today's day in age can be challenging, and Nathan understands that and challenges you to be more vulnerable in your walk. I love this book and highly recommend it to all."

Trevor Tyson, writer, speaker, and media personality

"*Good Man* is a dangerous title these days, yet the pursuit is as timeless and important now as it ever was. Nathan Clarkson's wrestling with what makes a man good, what makes him better tomorrow than he is today, is honest and invites us to do the same. In an age of mockery and skepticism, Clarkson seeks the complex nature of goodness with an earnestness and balanced optimism we could all learn from."

Sam Eldredge, coauthor of *Killing Lions*
and executive editor of *And Sons*

"I'm a mom of boys, and I love this book! Nathan's transparency is refreshing. *Good Man* will influence men to find value and self-worth in the One who created them, the One who calls them perfect, not by their doing but by the Savior who died on the cross for them, taking them from ordinary to extraordinary to be used no matter what their pasts looks like."

Shari Rigby, actress in *Overcomer*, author of *Beautifully Flawed*, and founder of The Women in My World

"I'm really proud of my friend for writing a book on what he aspires to be. But I'm even more proud of him for being honest about where he is at, because Nathan knows the deeper truth—to be who God desires us to be, we must be built on the truth that we are unconditionally loved as we are, God's beloved child."

David Leo Schultz, director of *Ragamuffin*, *Brennan*,
and *God's Fool*

GOOD MAN

An Honest Journey into Discovering Who
Men Were Actually Created to Be

Nathan Clarkson

BakerBooks

a division of Baker Publishing Group
Grand Rapids, Michigan

Published by Baker Books
a division of Baker Publishing Group
PO Box 6287, Grand Rapids, MI 49516-6287
www.bakerbooks.com

Printed in the United States of America

Library of Congress Cataloging-in-Publication Data
Library of Congress Cataloging-in-Publication Data
Names: Clarkson, Nathan, 1989– author.
Title: Good man : an honest journey into discovering who men were actually created to be / Nathan Clarkson.
Description: Grand Rapids : Baker Books, a division of Baker Publishing Group, 2020. | Includes bibliographical references.
Identifiers: LCCN 2019055541 | ISBN 9781540900234 (paperback)
Subjects: LCSH: Christian men—Religious life. | Men (Christian theology)
Classification: LCC BV4528.2 .C585 2020 | DDC 248.8/42—dc23
LC record available at https://lccn.loc.gov/2019055541

Published in association with The Bindery Agency, www.TheBinderyAgency.com

20 21 22 23 24 25 26   7 6 5 4 3 2 1

To my father, Clay, and my brother, Joel,
for showing me my entire life
what a good man looks like.

Contents

Introduction

Good Men Are . . .

I didn't really want to write a book titled *Good Man*.

Not because I don't think it's a worthy subject to engage with, but rather because I felt that my fears, faults, and failures disqualified me from even broaching the subject. I do long—and always have—to be a good man. But honestly, I don't always feel that I am one.

When my family or friends tell me, "You're a good man," I feel a twinge of guilt accepting the compliment, knowing the truth of who I really am: a struggling, broken man who wants to be good but fails more often than not.

But in looking through the Good Book in preparation for this project, I found that most of the people God used to build His kingdom and spread His message were flawed, imperfect, and constantly failing individuals.

Thomas was a doubter.

Peter was a liar.

David was an adulterer.
John the Baptist was crazy.
Paul was a murderer.

And so on and so forth. Each of these men had *huge* character flaws and moral failings, but the one thing I found in each of them was that despite their shortcomings, they had the want—a desire to grow, mature, and follow the call the Creator had for their lives.

And through this, through their stories of imperfectly following God, I discovered good men aren't perfect men. Being a good man isn't the absence of failing; instead, it's the determination to decide, and keep on deciding, to get up and continue on.

To keep fighting to become the men they were designed to be.

―――――――――――

When I hear the words *good man*, I am bombarded with mental images of what a good man might look like. Even if I begin with only the word *man*, my guess is that many things come to your mind.

"Real men work out." "Real men don't dance." "Real men hunt." "Real men can fight." "Real men drink beer, not wine." And the classic, "Real men don't cry."

But while many of these phrases are tongue-in-cheek, they affect us. Gradually, our definition of a man starts looking a lot like the stereotypes we've seen for decades.

Do you envision a bearded, muscle-bound, gun-shooting stoic with a cigarette in hand and whiskey on his breath? He's able to hunt, fight, and woo women with ease? Maybe he's a rich and charismatic businessman who's able to take from the world what he wants, showing only undeterred drive—never faltering. Or maybe he's a rock star, living a life of pleasure and fame, who does what he wants when he wants.

Perhaps these images stem from comic books, action movies, or video games, or perhaps they come from people we know. No matter where they come from, we all have ideas about what makes a man.

Then we add the word *good*. And with the term *good man*, we may envision images of even more refined and pressure-inducing men. Many of us might picture a pastor, spiritual leader, scholar, or "Christian celebrity." Someone constantly praying and quoting Scripture, able to withstand and deny any sort of temptation. He has a family and a college degree. He waited until marriage to have sex. He has a good job. He's a steady provider, and many applaud him for his polished life, inspiring Instagram feed, and unwavering goodness.

Maybe your images differ from mine, but either way, I'm willing to wager you have struggled with the feeling that you can't live up to what it means to be a good man.

For years I've struggled with both wanting to live up to my definition of a good man and wanting to give up when I fail.

———

For a long time, I've wrestled with this notion of what a good man is and how I can become one. Eventually, when it was evident the modern world didn't have the answers I was looking for, I turned to the Creator of men to see if maybe there, in His words, I could find a more satisfying and complete picture of who I was trying so hard to become.

I went back to God's Word and looked at what the Creator says. I went through history and looked at the men who made a positive difference in the world, and I looked at the men in my own life who I considered to be good men (there were not many). Then I began piecing together a new image of what a good man might truly be.

What I found in my search was a whole new image of what this man looks like. I found that it was never about how deep his voice was or how much he could bench press, the absence of mistakes or having life figured out, success or romantic prowess. Instead, it was about something much more real, deep, and difficult to attain.

Each man I looked at—whether from the Bible, history, or my own life—was very human. He struggled and failed. He had broken places in his heart and mind. Some were physically weak, and others fought addictions and moral failures. They didn't look alike; some had beards and low voices, some were clean shaven (crazy, I know), and some couldn't speak at all.

So often in Scripture I found that what makes a man is not his outward appearance but his inward heart position. His desire and dedication to pursue (even imperfectly) attributes that mimic God Himself, including unconditional love, generosity, wisdom, forgiveness, the list goes on. God says in the Old Testament, "Man looks at the outward appearance, but the LORD looks at the heart" (1 Sam. 16:7 NKJV).

This more elusive but authentic image of a good man is a far cry from the destructive and often toxic image of the "modern man" we have come to know. But that image is one we ought to leave behind us to take up a new one—a better, truer one.

I invite you to explore with me fifteen attributes that a good man must embody.

If I'm honest, I was scared to write this book, mostly because while I have always wanted to be a good man, I still struggle, fail, fall, and doubt.

But I'm so thankful that the definition of what a good man is, spoken from the Creator Himself, doesn't rely on me being perfect—just willing.

No matter who you are, where you're from, what's been done to you, or what you've done—you have the capacity to choose to live the design God has created, one that will ever so slowly shape you into the good man you were made to be.

Will you journey with me?

Adventurous

> My brothers. I see in your eyes the same fear that would take the heart of me. A day may come when the courage of men fails, when we forsake our friends and break all bonds of fellowship, but it is not this day. An hour of wolves and shattered shields when the Age of Men comes crashing down, but it is not this day! This day we fight! By all that you hold dear on this good earth, I bid you stand.
>
> Aragorn, *The Lord of the Rings: The Return of the King*

I can still remember the sting of cold air hitting my face as I threw open the laundry room door and stepped into my backyard. A sharp mountain wind blew off the plains and around my childhood house.

In my hand, I held a perfectly straight stick. I had carved one end into a point with my favorite pocketknife and tightly wrapped the other in twine, creating a handle. This was my sword. I squeezed it hard, my frigid fingers wrapped around

ded up the steep hill and into the mountains

recently seen my first PG-13–rated movie, *The Lord
Rings: The Fellowship of the Ring*, and there on a magical
ight in an old movie theater as the epic images of Middle-
earth swirled around me, I had suddenly known who I wanted
to be.

I was twelve, on the cusp of manhood—ready to leave behind
the boy I had been and step into the life of the warrior I had in
my heart. That day on the mountain I wore a Gap sweatshirt
that served as my armor, the hood my helmet, and as I reached
the top of a foothill, I caught my breath and looked out over
the ever-expanding view stretching as far as the eye could see
down the Rockies and into the endless western sky.

Then, as I turned around, my eyes fell upon my castle, perched
at the top of a nearby hill. Fashioned out of old, splintery ship-
ping pallets and leftover rope from our move, my castle overlooked our neighborhood. I approached it and crawled in carefully, ignoring the creaks and groans of the old wood. There I
prepared for the battle that lay ahead.

I could see my breath as I waited cross-legged on the cold,
hard floor. The yellow afternoon light beamed through the
cracks in the walls and bounced off the dust hanging in the
air. Out of the corner of my imagination, I saw a horde of dark
and ruthless enemies right outside my fortress, dawning the hill
and ready for battle. I took a deep breath as I drew my stick and
centered it between my eyes before I charged out of the castle.
I took the first mighty swing, beginning the fight by whirling
my sword with what I imagined were the skillful moves of a
trained ranger, one by one defeating the shadowy figures that
threatened all that was good. I fought until I was out of breath,

until the final imaginary enemy had fallen, and there I stood on the hill, victorious.

Now, sitting in my studio apartment almost eighteen years later, pushing thirty years old, I am forced to think about how far I've come from that boy I once was; I am no longer a chubby adolescent, but a six-foot-three, 230-pound man. My voice is deeper, and I have a beard.

I no longer play in rickety forts. I traded in my sharpened stick-swords for pens, and my imaginary enemies have become real-world struggles.

But as I think back, I realize that something is still lingering in my heart, something that was also present in me as a boy. As I close my eyes, letting my mind and heart wander, I find that the "something" is a strong and steady voice calling out to me, urging me to be a good and great man. It gives me a deep desire to use my life for something bigger than myself and to live out a true and epic story.

I wish I could say I've always listened to and followed the call, but life has a way of drowning it out with the noise of tedious work, mental illness, broken relationships, and unrealized dreams. But still, it's been there beckoning me—sometimes whispering, sometimes yelling—reminding me that I was made for more.

The voice that calls to me is the same one that spoke the universe into existence. It's the unchanging, ever-present, and timeless voice of my Creator calling out to the deepest parts of my being. And while I have wandered, stumbled, and fallen along the way, my Creator's voice still speaks. Even though I'm an imperfect and struggling man, it calls to me just as it did when I was a young boy fighting imaginary enemies, telling me I was created to be a good man. And I can be, should I only listen and obey.

The voice of God that calls my name calls to all of us, and He has been calling since the first man walked the earth. God is inviting us into the beautiful story He has waiting for us. The one He designed at the beginning of time that tells us who we are and who we were made to be: good men.

But what is a good man? Somewhere along the way we wandered away from the beautiful design we were made to live into—we walked away from the grand story that was written for us. And in doing so, we lost ourselves.

> We traded kindness for cruelty,
> peace for pride,
> servanthood for selfishness,
> love for lust,
> goodness for greed,
> hope for hate,
> and desire for despair.

Through the years, we have forgotten what makes good men and why we desperately need them. In the hubris of modern culture, we have left behind the ancient ways that were written for us thousands of years ago. But now, for the sake of the world, we must return to them.

———

We need only to take a quick look at our culture to see that men are in crisis.

- The rate of suicide among men continues to dramatically rise to almost four times that of women, being one of the leading causes of death for men under the age of forty-five, and almost half of men who have considered suicide haven't shared those feelings with anyone.[1]

- New statistics show a staggering 80 percent of teenage to adult men regularly view pornography, even though it has been heavily linked to increased rates of sexual dissatisfaction, divorce, sexual harassment, and even sexual assault. The average age of exposure to sexually explicit material is only eleven years old.[2]

- One study shows that 85 percent of domestic violence is committed by men and the vast majority of mass shootings, gang violence, and serial killings are perpetrated by males.[3]

Even beyond statistics, we can plainly see in our everyday lives our desensitization to violent music, movies, and video games. We've become accustomed to crude and misogynistic locker-room talk from our peers, comfortable with destructive masculinity. We are deadened to the shocking news of yet another abusive Hollywood figure being outed, a corrupt politician wielding his power for selfish gains, or even our beloved spiritual pillars getting caught in years of moral compromise.

Even as I write this, it feels overwhelming. What are we to do about this broken male culture that we are a part of? Are there good men left? Were there ever any to begin with? Is it even possible to be a truly good man?

The answer is yes.

The truth is, men of this generation have become passive, angry, selfish, predatory, violent, and bored. But that's not where the story has to end.

Men were designed by a good Creator with intent. We were made to be dedicated, peaceful, serving, protective, kind, and purpose driven.

It is clear that men were made for more, but we have lost our way down a dark and destructive path. Inside each of us is a longing for meaning, a yearning for greatness, and a search for truth. Because of the broken world we live in, we have lost our way.

But just like me at twelve years old, in the heart of every little boy and every grown man is a hero, the soul of a good man who has the capacity to bring life into his world, protect innocence, create beauty, seek truth, love deeply, laugh loudly, explore, discover, adventure, provide, help, heal, and worship his Creator.

It was the day of my thirteenth birthday. Finally, it had arrived. As I opened my eyes that morning, the world felt different. I was finally a man. I stood in the bathroom carefully gazing into the mirror at the pale, skinny-fat boy staring back at me. I flexed, hoping to magically see more muscle on my arms now that I was officially *not* a kid, but I found the same soft limbs I'd had the day before. I looked for facial hair around my jaw but saw nothing but skin. Even though not much had visibly changed in the course of the short eight hours that ushered me into young-adulthood, I could feel something shifting inside of me.

My mom called to me from the living room, interrupting my thoughts, to tell me to come downstairs. With one more look in the mirror, I shut off the lights and headed to the living room. Excitement in my steps took me around the corner, and there was my dad, holding a real, honest-to-goodness, gold-hilted, silver-bladed sword. It was just like the ones used by the heroes of Middle-earth, just like I had imagined in my backyard, but this was no sharpened stick.

My heart skipped a beat, and I quickly drew a breath. I took the sword, and as I wrapped my fingers around its hilt, I felt a strange sense of power and strength. With the gift came a speech, or perhaps an exhortation from a king to a knight, and my dad told me that this sword was to represent how I ought to see myself as I lived and moved in the world. I was to take on the identity of a warrior fighting for what was right, defending beauty, and protecting innocence. The sword was supposed to serve as a reminder of the responsibility that comes with strength.

But most of all, the sword was to be a symbol that I had been called out and invited into an epic story designed by my Creator. Should I listen and follow this call, I would find who I was created to be.

The sword now hangs in my childhood home in Colorado. So often I have come home after a long year and seen it as I opened the door to my old room, causing the devastating realization of how far I've strayed from those truths about myself and my calling. But still it hangs as a reminder of, or perhaps an invitation back into, the journey I began those many years ago. It's beautiful that no matter how far I've wandered from, forgotten, or failed to be the man I was made to be, God still calls to me. He asks me to listen to His voice ringing out from the deepest parts of who I am, to come back into the story He has for me to tell. And even at twenty-nine years old, I will wrap my fingers around the mighty sword's hilt, lift it up to my eyes, and once again imagine myself to be the hero I still have in my heart. The hero He created me to be.

———

Our Creator is calling all of us—every man. No matter who you are, where you're from, what you look like. No matter how big or small you are, what your education level is, how much money you make. No matter your IQ score, how old you are, what's been done to you, or what you've done, God is handing you the sword and inviting you into (or back into) His epic story to become who you were made to be . . . a good man.

Questions for Reflection

1. Have you ever felt the desire to be a good man, to live for something greater than yourself and be a part of an epic story? If so, when do you first remember feeling this?
2. What ways do you notice men falling short of who they were made to be both in popular culture and in your own life?
3. What do you think are some qualities a good man must possess?

> For the word of God is alive and powerful. It is sharper than the sharpest two-edged sword, cutting between soul and spirit, between joint and marrow. It exposes our innermost thoughts and desires.
>
> Hebrews 4:12

A PRAYER FOR
OUR JOURNEY

O God, who has before time seen and known us,
who has counted the hairs on our heads, who has
knitted us in our mothers' wombs, and who has
created a story for us to live and a path for us to
follow, help us hear Your calling on our lives. Let it
draw us to the beautiful and fulfilling path that leads
us toward You, our Creator, the giver of all life.

Let us not be distracted by the seductive voices of
the world but instead keep our eyes on the path
You have asked us to walk and our hearts on
the song You have composed for us to play.

May we take courage in Your love and grace as
we embark on the ancient way, the only one that
leads to true redemption and ultimate fulfillment.

Give us strength to keep going even when the
storms of life rage, and keep us ever in Your
sight as we seek to find who we were created
to be and the story we were made to tell.

Amen.

TWO

Devout

Being Christian is not the result of an ethical choice or a lofty idea, but the encounter with an event, a person, which gives life a new horizon and a decisive direction.

Pope Benedict XVI

The times I have experienced God's presence in a monumental and moving way are far fewer than I would like, but I return to those memories when I am struggling to feel God's breath or hear His voice. They are reminders to me of the real and visceral presence I have felt in those moments.

When I was thirteen, my family and I once camped out on the porch of our home, which sat at the side of the Rocky Mountains. Curled up in my sleeping bag next to my golden retriever, Penny, I fell asleep to the sounds of the hushed forest. Long after midnight, a cool breeze blew across my face, opening my eyes to a sight I can still vividly remember nearly twenty years later. As the sleep cleared from my eyes, I encountered above me a cloudless sky painted with a million shining galaxies, filled with dancing stars and shimmering planets. I was stunned in awestruck wonder. My trance was broken as a meteor silently flew by. Knowing this was a holy moment, I drew in a deep breath and captured a mental picture of the view that would stay etched in my mind forever. There in the 3:00 a.m. silence beneath a brilliant sky that seemed to be painted just for me, I knew I was looking at the handiwork of a master Creator. I knew I was looking at the artwork of God.

A few years later, I was at a concert by one of my favorite bands. It was a nice respite from the throes of teenagehood and what seemed like a never-ending war with my mental illness. I was hoping to drown out, for just a couple of hours, the unforgiving and incessant voices of obsessions, self-doubts, and insecurity that lived in my head. Loud concerts seemed to be a classic favorite of many young people in situations like mine. Toward the end of the show, covered in sweat and surrounded by screaming fans, the lead singer said he was going to play a song that was inspired by his struggle with his own demons. It was a song of redemption and freedom. As the ambient guitar notes soared to the towering roof over the venue and the powerful drums shook the ground, I could feel something in my feet that slowly made its way to my heart as the song progressed, until finally, with music blaring, I felt God's presence all around me while I screamed the words as if we were the only ones there. For a minute amid the chaos of my angsty teenage world, I felt His presence and love over me. I felt it so strongly, I didn't know if I wanted to laugh or cry. But He was there, and I knew.

Then in my twenties, on a cold New York day, my friend and makeshift tour guide, Lou, and I came across one of the many unlocked sanctuaries off a street on the Upper West Side. It had been a normal winter day in the city as we made our way through the avenues, when Lou said he wanted to show me something in a nearby church. I was hoping to catch my breath and warm up for a moment before continuing on our way. But when the wooden doors, beautifully carved with figures of the saints, opened before me and I stepped inside, I was confronted with something striking. I stopped and stood with my mouth agape, the sound of the closing doors echoing around me. A thirty-foot-tall crucifix hung over the fifty rows of pews. It was intricately sculpted and looked so lifelike that I had to blink.

Christ on the cross.

The figure in front of me was powerful. He felt real. His skin glowed in the yellow light from a sinking sun falling through the old stained-glass windows, and the blood on his ribs, seeming to shimmer with movement, looked like the wound had just happened. It was a sight from a story I had heard many times before as a pastor's kid, but seeing such a masterful rendering live and in the "flesh" in front of me, where the culmination of all the words I had heard were formed into a physical representation, affected me so deeply that the only word I could utter was *wow*.

I've read many books, heard a multitude of sermons, and sat through an endless number of youth group talks about what "godly behavior" does and doesn't look like. Most of them included a list of some sort or another, often containing classics like "Don't drink," "Don't swear," "Don't have sex before marriage," "Read your Bible every day," "Pray three times a day," and a host of other moral directives on how to be a good Christian.

And the thing is, I've always wanted to be a devout man of God. I've heard the stories of saints for so long—stories of men who would pray for hours a day to conquer their sins, weaknesses, and doubts; stories of men who would live in silence in the middle of the wilderness, simply meditating on great and spiritual things; stories of men seeing miracles happen at their hands; and stories of men talking to God like He was right there with them. I wanted to feel God like these men had. But it seemed this would only be possible for me if somehow, some way, I was able to do enough, pray enough, be good enough, and follow the directions from sermon notes and well-meaning Christian books.

Try as I might to be "devout," I simply could not conjure up enough effort and ability to be a true man of God. My want was and still is great, but my desire is often dimmed by the reality of my inconsistency, doubts, and failures that seem to point to me being more of a simple sinner than a faithful saint.

I had felt God. I knew He was there, and I knew I wanted to follow Him, but my feet were prone to tripping and my eyes to distraction. No matter how hard I tried, I simply couldn't live up to the spiritual practices and moral lists that seem required to earn the title of "man of God."

I wonder if you can relate. You want to be a man of God, someone people see as a picture of maturity, consistency, and stalwart faith, but the reality of being a sinful, broken, imperfect human seems too great a barrier to ever cross.

This, perhaps, is made even more difficult by living in a world that is not only indifferent to God but also actively angry at

Him and those who attempt to follow His voice. We live in a culture that mocks belief in the divine, scoffs at moral goodness, and laughs at the ones who claim to know Him.

―――――

What do I do? That's the question I ask myself. Do I give up and put my hope in the Sinner's Prayer, which offers little more than fire insurance, leaving the work of real spiritual devotion to the pros? Do I accept that maybe I wasn't cut out to be a devout man of God? I've thought that many times. *Why even try?* I ask myself. *What's the point if I'm just going to fall short?*

There's an old hymn found in tattered hymnals in almost every small-town church. I remember singing it as a kid in the very same chapel where stringent moral lists were preached and a droning, out-of-tune choir sang. Even at a young age, I was struck by the hymn's words, words that contrasted with the sermons I was hearing: "Prone to wander, Lord, I feel it, / Prone to leave the God I love."[1]

That's it! That's me. That's a lot of us. We so desire to love God with all we have but feel the weight of our imperfect humanity daily. Thinking back on those words I heard as a kid lets me know today that I'm not alone. There are men of God, just like the hymn writer from hundreds of years ago, that struggle. This realization led me to believe that perhaps being a man of God is less about a list of rules and more about a heart turned toward the Creator.

―――――

When I think of the dry moral lists found in sermons and books juxtaposed with the beauty and wonder I have experienced in God's presence beneath the stars, in beautiful music, and in stunning pieces of art—they don't even compare.

So often as humans we want to quantify, organize, and dilute an infinite, loving, and wondrous God into a formula we can understand or a list of rules we can follow. Sometimes we throw out God altogether, since it's easier to follow a few rules than it is an invisible and unpredictable God. But the beautiful thing about our God is that He doesn't just live on paper or in abstract ideas or through lofty concepts; He lives as a real person—speaking, breathing, moving. Remember how I felt Him so viscerally in my life, causing me to long for more. We all can experience a love for and devotion to Him that comes from our interacting with His real presence—a living God.

The God of everything didn't wait until we finally followed the instruction book correctly. Instead, He entered our world amid our mess to be with us. "Emmanuel" is what the early Christians called Jesus, and it means literally "God with us." Jesus spent most of His life with the imperfect but willing sinners—the prostitute who hadn't cleaned up her act, the tax collector who was still greedy, the fishermen who lived in pettiness and fear, and even the old Pharisee Nicodemus who longed for a God beyond a list of laws. But each of their lives was changed not because they were given a list of rules but because they had an encounter with a living, loving God. They were transformed not by their own effort but by a great and glorious God.

Creation is changed when it encounters its Creator.

Morality is needed and flows from God, but it is not God. Moral and healthy lives are beautiful by-products of knowing Him. If we wait to know God until we are perfect and completely morally upstanding, we will never know Him. It doesn't take being good to know God; we are made good by knowing God. Knowing my Creator inspires me to live as I was intended.

If we desire to live as we were created to live, we must be in connection with our Creator.

Practically speaking, to be a man of God—to be devout—we don't need to be moral enough or worthy enough or to look good enough or even do enough spiritual things. We need only to consistently put ourselves in places and moments where we can encounter God. In knowing and connecting with Him, we will find the true conduit to the growth, change, and godliness we so desire.

For me, that means talking to my Creator in the quiet darkness of my gym's steam room three times a week or whispering small prayers of thanks and requests for protection throughout my days. For you, perhaps that means taking a daily walk during which you can express the deepest parts of your heart and mind to God and see Him in nature. Or maybe that means riding in a car through the country or working where you can spend time conversing with God. Or maybe when you're alone in your room staring at the ceiling, you invite Him into your thoughts. Or maybe you go to a symphony, engage in a hobby, or talk to God before you close your eyes to fall asleep. Or perhaps you learn the intricacies of His nature by reading a chapter of His Word a day.

Because we are limited in our humanity, sometimes our efforts to commune with God won't always result in a waterfall of His presence like we might hope to experience, and sometimes we won't feel anything at all. But in learning to regularly pay attention to God's presence and reserve space and time to encounter Him even in our brokenness, we will find that, day by day and moment by moment, we are more filled with His wisdom, love, grace, and presence.

However you prefer to commune with God, know this: God isn't waiting until you are good enough to connect with you. Goodness, becoming a good man of God, will come only after you encounter Him right where you are.

Questions for Reflection

1. Do you sometimes feel you need to be "good" before you can go to God?

2. Do you think being a man of God is mostly about being moral? Do you believe there is more?

3. What are some ways you can begin experiencing and connecting with God more regularly?

> Because of his great love for us, God, who is rich in mercy, made us alive with Christ even when we were dead in transgressions—it is by grace you have been saved.
>
> Ephesians 2:4–5 NIV

THE MAN OF GOD

God of all, You know we long for You and to be
as David was—men after Your own heart.
We long to know You better and to
encounter Your presence every day.
We long to let our lives be a picture of
what these encounters can do.
Teach us to experience You and Your presence more.
Show us that we are made worthy and called sons
not because of our own merits but because of Yours.
Show us that we are made worthy not by our own actions
but because of what You have done.
Show us that we are loved not because of our
own goodness but because of Your goodness.
Open our eyes and ears to Your presence.
Teach us to recognize Your voice
and long for connection with You.
Help us want to want You more.
Make us men of God.

Amen.

THREE

Heroic

It's not who I am underneath, but what I do that defines me.

Bruce Wayne, *The Dark Knight*

Acting chose me more than I chose it. I realized at some point around eighteen, when I was looking at the rest of my life, that I had been playing pretend since I was a young boy. So when it came time to choose a direction for my life, I decided I simply didn't want to stop acting.

As a kid, I would run around my house in a cape, acting like a superhero. When my family did Bible reenactments, I would demand I play David in the Goliath story. One time I dressed up as American soldier and actor Audie Murphy, in real WWII military garb and everything, for a class speech. And while I played in my backyard box forts, in the recesses of my imagination I always chose to play the hero. Because that's who I wanted to be.

I've been acting professionally for over a decade. And one of the first things you learn as a young actor is your "type"—the kinds of characters you will best play. Typecasting is a necessary and sometimes frustrating reality of an actor's life. I had envisioned myself as the leading man "hero" type at one point, so it was an interesting moment when the first casting director I ever talked to told me that I would most likely play villains.

She wasn't wrong. In my first ever speaking role in a movie, I was a masked murderer, complete with an ax and a handgun. I then went on to play cult members, murder suspects, robbers, psychotic mental patients, and even your run-of-the-mill sexist frat boy.

While these roles were fun, and I couldn't complain about living my dream, I still desired to be a hero.

Since casting directors obviously hadn't gotten the memo, one day I decided to write my own story. I sat down and typed out a script, ninety pages, each one filled with the story of the hero I would someday play. The movie has yet to be made. But I wrote it because that's who I want to be and what I will always be working toward. I knew the story I wanted to tell.

———

Stories are powerful. They have the unique ability to change, teach, and inspire us in ways that nothing else can. Jesus changed the entire world with His stories, and God gave us His Word as a collection of stories.

Since the dawn of humankind, stories have appeared on cave walls in the form of crudely scribbled pictures, weaving their way into every known historical culture in all corners of the world. And we are ever learning and perfecting new and different ways of telling stories, even now, thousands of years later.

We have an entire industry dedicated to their creation. Hollywood produces billions of dollars' worth of stories each year because we continue to flip open our laptops, turn on our flat-screen TVs, and gather in old movie theaters with aged felt seats, stale popcorn, and overpriced tickets to lose ourselves in a narrative, even if only for a few hours.

It's like our hearts and minds are hardwired to respond to stories—an internal drive that keeps us looking for and engaging with narratives outside our own. Something in the makeup of humanity allows us to see ourselves in the story line and empathize with the characters.

Growing up, my favorite stories were about Superman. Something about how steadfast, strong, and good he was drew me in and captured my mind as a boy. His crimson cape and steely stare ignited something in my young heart. I plastered posters of him around my room, reminding me that there was a way to live as a hero in my own world just as he did in his. I was able to see myself as a hero in my own story.

Superman might have been fighting evil masterminds who were determined to destroy the world, but as I read those pages, I was given the strength and inspiration to fight my own enemies of mental illness, learning disabilities, and boyhood struggles.

That's what good stories do. They not only entertain us but also serve as a parallel to our lives and an inspiration to live in our heroes' footsteps.

But having lived in Hollywood for the better part of a decade, I've noticed a disturbing and unsettling trend. The heroes are disappearing. We once had a myriad of strong characters with unshakable morals and inspiring lives who we were able to look to and align ourselves with. As culture has moved into an age where we actually celebrate selfishness, greed, pride, arrogance, and subjective morality, we see the landscape of our modern stories becoming more and more void of good and true fictional figures.

We've traded the virtue of Superman, the upright strength of Aragorn, the moral dedication of Luke Skywalker, and the virtuous intellect of Sherlock Holmes for the corruption of Frank Underwood, the vitriol of Walter White, the violent cynicism of Deadpool, and the selfish, misogynistic hedonism of Don Draper. We have allowed our heroes to be replaced by "antiheroes" who, upon further inspection, might just be straight up villains.

These antiheroes enable us to connect with the more broken parts of ourselves without the pressure to rise above them and live up to an impossible image. These kinds of characters encourage us to live into and revel in the worst parts of ourselves, giving us allowance to sink lower into a comfortable mire where goodness is seen as something that merely gets in the way of our getting what we truly want.

But perhaps that's the problem: comfort. These antiheroes ask nothing of us. They don't inspire us toward our better selves or push us to examine and work on our flaws. They invite us to revel in them. They tell us the ends justify the means, what we want is the most important thing, and nothing is more important than our wants.

Don't get me wrong. I love complicated and morally nuanced characters, and I have thoroughly enjoyed some of the films and shows I listed. But still, I worry that we are losing something when we trade classic and upright characters for corrupt and self-serving ones. I worry because the stories of any culture both inspire and are inspired by the hearts of men, and if we have only negative examples of how to live, void of any challenge to embrace virtue and goodness, I'm forced to wonder who we already are and who we are becoming.

———

The questions I get asked most as an actor are "What's your favorite movie?" and "If you could play any role, what would it be?"

For a long time, I would think through what answer would make me sound most unique, relevant, and cool, naming pretentious Oscar winners in hopes of being seen as a "real" actor. But in the interest of transparency, my truthful answer is something less cool and far more cliché: Batman.

When the film *The Dark Knight* came out in 2008, there seemed to finally be a hero on the big screen, Bruce Wayne, who had fears, failures, and doubts but *also* overcame them, fought for what was right, and strived to do good in his world. For the first time in a long time, I could connect with a character on an imperfect human level while simultaneously being inspired to live out the life of a hero.

But another character in that movie stole the show—the Joker, Batman's arch nemesis who threatens all that is good and pure with chaos and destruction. The Joker is played brilliantly by one of my favorite actors, Heath Ledger. His performance perfectly captures the nihilistic, chaotic, destructive, and violent mentality any good villain should have.

But when the movie came out, a strange phenomenon happened. Bruce Wayne, or Batman—the hero the movie was named after—took a back seat to the Joker.

Perhaps it was the infamous villain's careless and untouchable swagger all of us guys wish we had that drew so many young men to his altar. Maybe it was that he did what he wanted when he wanted, which is appealing to our darker sides. Or maybe it was simply because he was bound by nothing—no moral code, no virtuous expectations, no relational pitfalls—making him seemingly impervious to life.

Even I was attracted to the alluring freedom of the Joker's cavalier, nothing-can-touch-me attitude. And it seemed like a lot of young men who were angry with life and fed up with being told what to do, falling short of societal expectations, and facing the chaos of a fractured world did too.

At the time, most of us thought little about the phenomenon and left well enough alone. But then on a warm and peaceful evening on July 20, 2012, a villain came to life and killed twelve people in cold blood in a movie theater in my home state of Colorado. James Holmes, the Dark Knight shooter, dressed as his favorite villain, the Joker, using a story and character as fuel for his own sad, selfish, and violent narrative, took the lives of a dozen people and injured dozens more.

While there might be fewer good, pure, and inspiring stories being made, and they might not be as popular, cool, or relevant in this modern age—stories matter. The characters and narratives we engage with *will* change us, for better or worse.

————

A good man has a responsibility to search for, connect with, and perhaps even create good stories.

Because the reality is, we are stories. The choices we make and actions we take here on this earth make up the movie of our lives. And only we decide what kind of story that is. If we truly want to be good men, to be the hero, to live a movie worth telling, we must identify the shaping narratives that we can align ourselves with. We must choose the ones that encourage us to live greater and more beautiful lives, protecting others, showing us the truth, and inspiring us to live as better characters in our own stories.

Questions for Reflection

1. Do you agree that stories have the power to shape and change us? Why or why not?

2. What stories did you grow up with (and even engage with now) that inspired and connected with you the most? What was it about them that you connected with?

3. What stories do you think might have a positive impact on you and the men of our culture today? What stories do you think might have a negative impact? Why?

> He told many stories in the form of parables, such as this one:
>
> "Listen! A farmer went out to plant some seeds. As he scattered them across his field, some seeds fell on a footpath, and the birds came and ate them. Other seeds fell on shallow soil with underlying rock. The seeds sprouted quickly because the soil was shallow. But the plants soon wilted under the hot sun, and since they didn't have deep roots, they died. Other seeds fell among thorns that grew up and choked out the tender plants. Still other seeds fell on fertile soil, and they produced a crop that was thirty, sixty, and even a hundred times as much as had been planted! Anyone with ears to hear should listen and understand."
>
> His disciples came and asked him, "Why do you use parables when you talk to the people?"
>
> Matthew 13:3–10

THE HERO

Righteous God, maker and source of
everything true, good, and just,
help us better align our lives to Yours.
Show us what true self-sacrifice means and how
to better live it in the world You've created.

Give us the desire to learn what is right and hate what
is evil, as well as the ability to never call one the other.
Give us the courage to fight for goodness in
the way You have so perfectly exemplified,
even if no one else fights with us.

Show us the value of truth, peace, love, and
innocence. Help us practice, in small ways, the choice
of the hero, laying down our lives for something
greater so that when much is asked of us, we
will be ready and willing to answer the call.

Thank You that in our struggle for
good we never struggle alone.
Help us be the heroes You have created us to be.

Amen.

FOUR

Honest

God, grant me the serenity to accept the things I cannot change, the courage to change the things I can, and the wisdom to know the difference.

Reinhold Niebuhr

Hi, I'm Nathan.

I have been prideful and egocentric while simultaneously being full of self-doubt and insecurity.

I have used sexuality in unhealthy ways.

I have struggled with lust and looking at things I shouldn't on screens.

I have used substances like alcohol and nicotine as an escape.

I have had a dysfunctional relationship with food, and I have deep insecurities about my body.

I have started fights, and I have let my anger get the better of me.

I have said deeply cutting things to people I love.

I have harshly criticized people I don't even know.

I have judged others while blindly ignoring my own faults.

I have lived my entire life with severe mental illness and learning disabilities.

I have considered suicide multiple times in my life.

I have yelled at God in anger, while completely ignoring all His direction, insight, and love.

These aren't fun or easy things to admit, much less record in permanent ink in this book. Like a scarlet tattoo for the entire world to see, the admissions may cause people to treat me differently, judge me harshly, or ultimately see past the "good Christian kid" identity I want to be known by. But even more than that, facing these parts of myself makes me feel weak and vulnerable. Given all these realities about myself, I sometimes think I shouldn't be writing a book about being a good man.

Because why should I? Why should someone who is flawed and imperfect write a book about being good?

That's a question I often ask myself.

But when I stand before my Creator in quiet times, soul laid bare, naked in my fractured humanity, where it is just God and me, I hear Him whisper, letting me know that it is only when I choose to acknowledge my brokenness to myself, others, and Him that I begin the process of becoming whole.

I remember sitting across from a thirtysomething pastor. He was the leader of a small community I had become a part of almost a year before. I had found this community at a time in my life when I needed one. I had just moved back to a big city and in the insecurities and uncertainty of an unseen future, I was grateful to have people to love and be loved by. We were sitting in the same room where our small group gathered every Wednesday night to talk, laugh, and connect, but that day the room had an entirely different aura. There were no chuckles or lighthearted conversation. No hugs or grins. I could hear the echo of my sinking stomach as I forced out the words I had to speak, knowing I could lose something I held so dear.

I told him I knew what was going on. His head sunk down and his eyes found the floor.

When I first joined, I quickly became close to many people in our small group and garnered their trust. Eventually, multiple women I had grown close to felt safe confiding in me. One woman in the group told me she had been sexually assaulted by the leader. I was shocked and angry. A cancer was growing right beneath the blemishless skin of this community.

The woman had trusted the pastor—a leader she saw as a "brother" who called himself a man of God. He posted Bible verses on his Instagram and sang worship songs in his car. But he had used his position of authority to prey on a vulnerable young woman, shattering her trust in him by propositioning, groping, and forcing himself on her.

When I told him what I knew, when he was faced with what he had done, he raised his eyes after a tense and heavy silence and told me this: He said it was the woman's fault because once she had asked him to sit next to her at a holiday party. He stated that even though she had said no multiple times to his advances, her earlier invitation for him to sit next to her at the party was reason enough to push past her protests. He said that if she didn't like it, she could leave the group. He said that it wasn't that big of a deal. She had been asking for it, and he had consumed too much alcohol and had just read some signals wrong, so no big deal.

After he said all of that, he was done. He had nothing else to say.

My face was twisted with pain and anger. I stared at my pastor as he fidgeted uncomfortably, his body betraying the truth of his words. His attempt to avoid, evade, and absolve himself from his guilt was pitiful, like a dog with its tail between its legs, trying to hide the soiled spot on the carpet.

How could someone who claimed to be a man of God so blatantly and maliciously dodge, blame, and ignore the reality of his actions—actions that caused deep pain to multiple lives, lives he was supposed to protect?

Doing my best to contain my thoughts and feelings, I quietly said my piece, got up, and walked out the door and out of a community I had come to know and love. I resolved that when confronted with mistakes I had made in the past or might make in the future, I would be different.

When confronted and shown the ugly truth of our actions, we may be tempted to respond by evading blame and any consequences. It can play out in the following ways:

We pass the blame. We try to find a way to frame our destructive actions so they aren't actually our fault; that really, we're not to blame for what we did. We say things like "She led me on," "I couldn't help it," "He should have done something differently," or the classic we learn as toddlers, "They started it."

We downplay. We minimize our behavior to escape the full ramifications of our actions. We try to convince ourselves and others that it wasn't *that* big of a big deal. We tell people to stop overreacting. We search for ways to dilute the truth so it's more palatable. We want to justify our behavior so that we won't have to face the full reality of who we are and what we've done.

We avoid. Sometimes we try to escape and ignore our destructive actions altogether. We lie to ourselves and others, hoping the consequences will go away. We think that if we can keep it to ourselves, keep it quiet, then maybe it will all just disappear. But it doesn't.

We see people behaving this way all the way back to the first man, Adam.

Adam was given paradise to live in, complete with a beautiful woman with whom to be fruitful and multiply in a garden with everything they could possibly want. God gave Adam only one stipulation: not to eat the forbidden fruit from one tree that was reserved for God. But like all of us, he quickly became discontented with what God had given him and wanted what was not his. Adam wanted control. So, infamously, Adam and his bride, on the suggestion of the devil himself, partook of the off-limits fruit. Immediately, Adam realized what he'd done. Genesis 3:7 says, "At that moment their eyes were opened, and they suddenly felt shame at their nakedness."

Being found out feels like being naked. Our hidden selves are exposed, and we will do anything to take cover and hide.

But God walked through the garden, knowing what Adam had done. Adam hid, but like all our secrets that we hope to keep in the shadows, God knows, and His light will reveal them.

Upon finding Adam, God asked, "Have you eaten from the tree whose fruit I commanded you not to eat?" (Gen. 3:11).

It's here in this story that we see the first fallen man, for the first time, engage and act out the systematic pattern of passing the blame, downplaying, and avoiding.

The first thing Adam did was hide, hoping to outsmart the all-seeing God and avoid the impending consequences, sure that if he could just conceal his mistake, like he had covered his nakedness, it would all be fine.

Then when God found him (because He always has and always will find us), Adam shifted the blame, cowardly telling God it was Eve's fault. It was her doing that made him act. Perhaps he was hoping he could avoid God's judgment by passing it off on a woman.

Then, Adam was quiet.

God responded.

> Since you listened to your wife and ate from the tree
>   whose fruit I commanded you not to eat,
> the ground is cursed because of you.
>   All your life you will struggle to scratch a living
>   from it.
> It will grow thorns and thistles for you,
>   though you will eat of its grains.
> By the sweat of your brow
>   will you have food to eat
> until you return to the ground
>   from which you were made.
> For you were made from dust,
>   and to dust you will return. (vv. 17–19)

God laid out the very real ramifications of Adam's actions, because nothing is hidden from God. Choices have tangible and weighty consequences.

Jesus, the new Adam, the second man without sin, who instead of falling to temptation overcame it, later told His followers,

> For all that is secret will eventually be brought into the open, and everything that is concealed will be brought to light and made known to all. (Luke 8:17)

There is deep and meaningful truth to be found in the story of Adam and Eve. Adam reaped eternal and long-lasting consequences because of his unwillingness to face what he had done.

The truth is, our actions have consequences. Even if we hide from everyone in our lives, God sees and knows.

———

Not wanting to own up to our mistakes, shortcomings, failures, and faults is natural and something all of us deal with. I wish I could say I would have acted differently than Adam did in Eden, but in all likelihood, I would have done the same thing. I fail and fall constantly. I choose my own way, taking a big ole juicy bite out of the forbidden fruit in my own life. Then, with a juice-stained face, convicted and confronted with my rebellious choices, I immediately want to hide and shift blame.

In Romans 7:19, Paul writes that he keeps doing what he doesn't want to do, and he can't do what he wants to. Have you been there? Have you ever tried and tried to do the right thing only to fail over and over again? I have, and sometimes it seems like there's no way out.

But there's good news. We don't have to hide, we don't have to blame, we don't have to downplay and be stuck in the real and heavy consequences of our mistakes. There's a better way.

It's the only way we can ever be free, but it's harder than hiding and blaming.

Our Creator has graciously offered us an out, and to get it we must do this: own up.

We have to recognize, realize, and take responsibility for what we've done. We have to admit our shortcomings and give them to Him. In return, He gives us a new way forward—one that will bring healing to our past, wisdom to our present, and hope to our future.

I struggled with things at nineteen that I am still fighting at twenty-nine.

But after more than a decade of facing my demons, I keep learning the hard lesson that to begin the process of overcoming my struggles, I must own up to the broken pieces of my life. Owning up is not something I can avoid on this journey. In fact, it might be one of the most important things I do, which could be the reason it's so hard.

Until we admit we are wounded and broken, the Doctor cannot begin His work. And, yes, surgery is painful, but ultimately, it's the only way we'll ever be whole.

Toward the end of Jesus's days here on earth, the New Testament details the stories of two men who made strikingly similar mistakes but had drastically different endings.

One betrayed Jesus and one denied Him.

I'm thinking of Judas and Peter. Both were Jesus's disciples—men who walked, talked, and lived with Christ—and both were fallible, broken men. Judas famously betrayed his master Jesus for thirty pieces of silver, handing Jesus over to the authorities to eventually be killed. Peter, when confronted by a crowd, denied ever having known Jesus for fear that he would be killed. But the interesting part is what happened *after* these men made their history-altering mistakes.

When confronted by Jesus, Peter fell to his knees, recognized his failure, and begged for forgiveness. In return, Jesus blessed him and made him one of the most revered leaders of His church.

Judas, upon realizing what he'd done, ran away and hid from Jesus, refusing to own his grievous mistakes. He ended up hanging himself and probably having his eyes pecked out by birds.

Both these men made mistakes. But one owned up and humbled himself and found blessing; the other hid and blamed and found death. The truth is, not owning our mistakes hurts no one more than ourselves. God so desires to heal, restore, and redeem our darkest hours and deepest regrets, but until we stop hiding, blaming, and pretending, He can't begin the process of making us new.

We are all born with the cancer of sin. We can see it every day in our thoughts, words, and actions. But until we accept the fact that we need help, we will not find healing.

———

Every Saturday I get into my car and drive out of Los Angeles to a small office beneath the Pasadena mountains, where I sit on a large couch in a small room and talk to my counselor, Jeff. I unload all my fears, faults, and failures. I tell him everything. Even the things that hurt, embarrass, and shame me.

And with all the broken pieces of my life exposed, with God's help, we begin to piece together the fragments in a new, healthy, and more beautifully integrated way.

I have been doing this for years, and as a result of therapy, I have watched myself grow in ways I never thought I would, think in ways I didn't know were possible, and heal in ways I thought were hopeless. But this is possible only because I have learned the power of being honest with myself and others.

———————

God tells us to confess our sins to one another, reminding us it's necessary for living a whole and beautiful life. But we live in a world where taking blame and owning up to a mistake is seen as weakness. Admitting we are wrong or we have acted badly is so often met with not only public but also personal shame and separation.

We have a desire to be competent and put together, strong and independent, pretending we don't make mistakes or finding a way to remove, lessen, or transfer fault when we do. Just as that pastor did when confronted with his own grievous actions. And I get it, because so often I want to cover up my sin too.

Because we're human, born into a broken world, we all have a dark thread of brokenness woven into our humanity—every last one of us, even our parents and our pastor. Destruction lives in the heart of every person.

But the beautiful thing about connecting to and knowing our Creator is that He loved us enough to die a painful and humiliating death just so we would have a way forward. A way past our mistakes and through our brokenness. And while this is a free gift, it requires us to accept that we need it. It requires us to own up.

Questions for Reflection

1. Why do you think owning up to our fears, faults, and failures is necessary for living a whole and fulfilling life?
2. What are you tempted to do when confronted with the ways you've messed up?
3. What are some things in your life you feel you need to own up to so you can begin the journey toward becoming a whole and healthy man?

> But if we confess our sins to him, he is faithful and just to forgive us our sins and to cleanse us from all wickedness.
>
> 1 John 1:9

THE REPENTANT

O great Creator, we come humbly before You, fully acknowledging that You are God and we are not. We recognize that You are perfect in all Your ways and we are broken and in need of Your forgiveness and grace.

We recognize that we have willingly gone our own way and rebelliously sought to be our own kings, and in so doing we've added to the fracture of an already broken world.

In both our actions and our inaction, we have caused destruction to ourselves and others, so we repent and ask for Your mercy with expectancy as You have taught us.

We vow to make right the situations and relationships we have had a hand in hurting, and we ask for Your wisdom in bringing about healing and wholeness through You to the world.

We are grateful that through Your promises of forgiveness, grace, and love, we have a way forward. One that leads us from brokenness to beauty, from hurt to healing, from regression to redemption.

Amen.

FIVE

Brotherly

Because our expression is imperfect we need friendship
to fill up the imperfections.

G. K. Chesterton

Once a month I gather with a small group of men in a backyard that sits atop a cliff overlooking a sparkling California
valley. We drive just fifteen miles outside the glitz of the harsh
lights of Hollywood, each of us making our way from our jobs,
families, and homes to gather around a roaring fire together.

Like King Arthur's Knights of the Round Table, we each
find our seat—an old camp chair, a piece of lawn furniture, or
a stump—as the warm firelight dances on our faces and sparks
gently fly into the smog of the nearby city.

At a glance we would appear to have little in common. We
are black and white men, old and young men, wealthy and poor
men, but men nonetheless, gathering for a purpose larger than
the outward trappings we bear.

For the first hour we sit and talk, connecting, laughing, eating, drinking, and sharing in life together.

We call the group The Firepit, and it was started by my good friend and mentor, Guy. He is a renaissance man and friend to all. He is also a dad of four boys and has a heart for men, connection, faith, and community. He started the group to give men of faith living and working in a lonely city a chance to be encouraged, to connect, and to know they aren't doing life alone.

After the laughing and talking has died down, we all find ourselves gazing at the fire in a more contemplative posture. Guy asks each of us in the circle to share the joys and trials of our lives. So, one by one, each man takes a few minutes to share his life, his dreams, his triumphs, his doubts, and his struggles.

It's interesting, sharing the intimate and personal parts of your life, being vulnerable and opening yourself up to a group of diverse men. But it's beautiful to see what happens: men being supported and loved in the midst of pain, challenges, weakness, and joy. This is not your typical squeaky-clean Bible study or polished Sunday service. It's incredibly raw and unmistakably real.

When it's my turn, I can feel a twinge of nervous energy as I mentally and emotionally face the fear that comes with opening myself up to the men around me. "Hey, guys, my name is Nathan," I say, keeping my eyes on the flames.

"Hello, Nathan," the group says back in a slightly off-tune baritone.

Then I carefully but confidently share my life with the men around me. I share what I'm happy about, what I'm struggling with, what I'm hoping for, and what I'm trying to heal from. I don't do this because it's comfortable, I do it's because it's cathartic, healthy, and good.

I finish and am met with a chorus of "Thanks, Nathan," and I look to the man to my right, signaling to him that it's his turn to share his life with the group.

After we have all finished, Guy prays and we lift up the men, our worries, and our wonder with strength, confidence, and care to a God who is present with us around the bonfire. There's nothing magical about doing this, nothing that fixes all the problems in my life or takes away the everyday struggles. But afterward, I walk out to my car feeling a bit lighter, more hopeful, less alone, and I carry a greater sense of purpose back into the life I have been called to.

My older brother, Joel, and I are completely different. Joel is introverted, methodical, and caring. I am passionate, outspoken, and independent. Joel is a musician who thoughtfully composes musical masterpieces for films and concerts. I am an actor who passionately performs in front of the camera. The stories of brothers being different are not new. From Cain and Abel to Caleb and Aron Trask, the narrative of brothers at odds as a result of their differences is a classic one. My brother and I have had our fair share of, shall we say, rousing debates.

But other narratives reveal a different reality—they show the strength of the bond between brothers, despite their differences. We see this in the lives of people like Louis Zamperini, who overcame the horrors of being a POW in WWII with the help of his brother, Pete; and Jesus's disciples Peter and Andrew, who, despite their differences, went on to change the world with God's message.

When it came to my brother and me, my parents knew they had two very different boys on their hands, so they intentionally and purposefully taught us not only to independently live our lives but to love and appreciate our differences, to seek out connection and shared values. We created a bond and a brotherhood by playing video games together, my brother patiently teaching me to ride a bike, and standing up for each other when one of us was being bullied. Now, as we are both grown men living our lives on different sides of the world, I know at any time I can call on my brother for anything and he can call on me. Because of a bond that's deeper than our differences, we walk through this life supported and connected.

Brotherhood isn't about fitting a mold, being exactly alike, or fitting in. It's about encouraging, building up, and supporting one another to become the men God created us to be.

———

There's a classic picture of a man that's weaved itself into our culture and my mind. It's of a stoic, silent, drifter type. He's hardened and cool, and he does life on his own terms, beholden to no one. And as much as I hate to say it, I like this guy. I often want to be him. I don't really like the thought of needing anyone or asking for help. If I could have it my way, I would be totally self-sufficient, independent, and "free."

There have been combined years of my life when I have chosen to do life alone and isolated from community, mentors, and support. At the time, I thought I was doing the right thing by pulling myself up by my bootstraps, being a man, and dealing with my problems myself.

It was more comfortable and felt safer this way, not opening myself up to having my actions, inner thoughts, and brokenness observed and critiqued by those around me. Both my happiness and my hardships were loads I bore alone.

As time went on, I slowly but surely began to grow weary of the secret wars in my mind and the silent struggles that come with living in a broken world. Bearing the entire weight of my burdens alone was too much, and I began to develop habits, hang-ups, and destructive patterns just to cope.

Following only my voice, I got lost and more lost, like a driver trying to navigate without a map in the dark. I thought I was free, not beholden to anyone else. I thought it was better and safer to do life alone. But it turned out to be hard, hurtful, and destructive. It was never the way I was intended or designed to live.

It might seem easier to live a life of self-reliance—needing only to worry about ourselves, doing what makes us happy, and hiding our sensitivities. But such isolation means we don't have the privilege of allowing someone to worry about us, the rewarding responsibility of serving others and experiencing camaraderie, or the healing act of sharing the personal parts of our lives with others who will celebrate the good times and unconditionally love us through the bad.

Sharing life is hard. Revealing personal parts of ourselves is uncomfortable, even painful. But it's a pain that will save us, heal us, and enable us to walk in strength, wisdom, and joy. We weren't made to be this solitary picture of a man all too many of us carry.

In his 1624 work titled *Devotions upon Emergent Occasions*, John Donne writes, "No man is an island, entire of itself; every man is a piece of the continent, a part of the main," meaning that on our own, we are not whole. We need community. Men were made to do life with other men. Humanity is intrinsically communal, meaning God designed us to need each other—not in a codependent, needy way, but in an interdependent, strength-giving, supportive way.

Paul the apostle often referred to the other leaders of the early church as brothers, and not without reason. He knew the absolute necessity of living in familial communion. In 1 Corinthians 12:12–27, he compared the body of Christ (the church) to a human body, each of us a different part: some are hands, some are legs, others are eyes or ears, but all are needed and all are reliant on one another to be fully effective.

———

Not long ago, I made a last-minute decision to go on an adventure for my twenty-eighth birthday. I got on a plane with only a backpack and headed on a trip that would take me to four countries in the course of a few days, ending in Oxford, England.

If you don't know much about Oxford, it is the location of one of the oldest universities in the world and where some of the greatest minds in literature, science, and culture originated.

Off an old cobblestone road outside of the main town is a pub called The Eagle and Child. It blends in and doesn't look much different from the hundreds of other public houses scattered across the small city. And it has all the same features of the watering holes of the area—old wood, low lights, and background music muffled by the murmurs of the locals. But this pub is special, for it's where the Inklings met.

The Inklings were a small group of writers, philosophers, and thinkers who gathered many years ago. The group had a few prominent figures, most notably (and my personal favorites) C. S. Lewis and J. R. R. Tolkien. They would gather at The Eagle and Child each week and, with a drink in hand, talk, share, debate, yell, laugh, and commune. These men were some of the most influential minds of the last one hundred years. Their thoughts and ideas, the very ones they sat and shared weekly, have reached tens of millions of people around the world. I have to wonder if it was those hours spent sipping drinks and sharing their souls in an old pub on the outskirts of town that propelled those men to greatness.

———

Even Jesus, the Son of God, didn't do life alone.

When He was beginning His ministry, He called twelve men around Him to share in the work of redeeming hearts. He lived with them, ate and cooked with them, laughed, fought, and cried with them, and in doing so, He changed the course of history.

Being in community can be hard. It can be frustrating and tiring, as it involves doing life with imperfect, messy, irrational, emotional humans. But I believe with all my heart that it's absolutely necessary on this journey to becoming good men.

We need the space to work out our struggles and get perspective and input that will help us see life and ourselves more clearly. For us to walk this path well, we need places where we can laugh loudly, talk deeply, and share openly.

The times in my life that I have experienced the most growth, strength, and health have been when I was walking with other brothers who were doing the same—when I was being supported and supporting others.

It was in the nights I sat with my high school best friends Matt, Chad, and Ben in a hot tub in the snow-covered landscape of Colorado until 3:00 a.m., talking about life, love, and God. It was the countless hours my friend Lou and I walked the streets of New York City, sharing our hurts, hopes, and inside jokes while giving support and levity for the lives we both led. It was the "Boys' Nights Out" as a kid, when my dad would take me and my brother out once a week, and over a meal, we would talk about what it means to be a godly man. It was the talks around campfires and in corners of bars, the laughter at movie nights with my roommates, and the long drives just listening to music and singing out loud with my brother. It was the nights in LA spent around a campfire with diverse men, with whom I could be open and exchange support amid a hard time in a hard city. It was every moment when I felt the freedom to share my life with the good men who were on the journey with me.

Questions for Reflection

1. Do you feel the need and/or desire to be in community and relationship with other good men? Why or why not?

2. When are the times you feel yourself wanting to do life alone? Does it work long term? Why or why not?

3. What are some ways you can begin to invest in friendships with other men of character in your life?

As iron sharpens iron,
    so a friend sharpens a friend.

Proverbs 27:17

A PRAYER FOR
BROTHERHOOD

God, who is inherently relational and knowable, we pray that in Your footsteps You would lead us to others looking to You so we would not walk alone on this path of life.

We ask that You bring about true and lasting friendships, and that in them we would find comfort, camaraderie, connection, communion, and accountability for the journey we are all on.

We pray that our hearts would be willing to be a friend to those who have none and that we would be humble enough to accept the love and friendship of others when we are alone.

Let us learn what true discipleship means in the context of close and life-giving relationships. Let us find mutual purpose in our lives and seek to help our brothers as they help us.

Let us never be taken by the lie that we can do life alone, and instead be persistent in searching for the community and connection we were created for.
Amen.

SIX

Healthy

Health is a state of complete mental, social, and physical
well-being, not merely the absence of disease or infirmity.

World Health Organization, 1948

I want six-pack abs like the guys on the cover of men's magazines, bulging biceps like the UFC fighters on TV, and pecs
you can bounce bullets off like Henry Cavill in *Man of Steel.*

Maybe it's because I love superhero movies and still have
multiple pictures of a comically ripped Superman on the walls
of my childhood bedroom. But whenever I get a glimpse of
myself in the mirror or see a shirtless photo of me at the pool,
I juxtapose that image with the latest Avengers hero covered in
muscles and realize just how super I am not.

Living in Hollywood can be daunting if you have physical
insecurities. It's a city with an industry that worships bodies.
Not all bodies—just the more chiseled and sculpted ones.

Our appearance-conscious culture, which worships physical perfection in magazines and on social media and reality
TV, leaves us feeling like no matter what we do, we'll never be
beach-body ready. So why not just embrace the "dad bod" and
call it a day? Why should we even worry about our bodies when
it's our hearts and minds God cares about?

———————

I remember being mad. It had been a fun night with friends at
a little get-together in a small New York City apartment. After
most of the people had left, I stayed behind to help clean up,
when one of my friends made a comment about how it looked
like I had gained a considerable amount of weight. He was con-
cerned. I didn't take it well. Criticism to me is kryptonite, and
I responded with some snarky comments that ultimately shut
him up and soothed my fractured ego. Or so I thought.

As I walked home in the glow of the city street lights, I felt
the buzz of the night fade into solitary silence. It haunted me
with the ghosts of past failures, frustrations, and loneliness. My
friend's words hung in my mind, tapping at my ego, reminding
me of one more thing I was failing at.

It had been a hard week, or really, a hard two years. I had
moved across the country to NYC after a couple of devastating
breakups, and I was clumsily trying to put my life back together.
But it was slow going, and I often found myself in a dark place,
looking to ease the depression that seemed to sneak in daily
with things that felt good for a moment but ultimately hurt
me. I had chosen not to drink alcohol during that time, as I
didn't want to find myself depending on it, but being human,
I found other ways to be physically self-destructive in an effort
to ease the pain—primarily eating and smoking. I told myself it

wasn't a big deal, at least I wasn't getting drunk. But more and more, as the healing got hard, I would turn to a quick puff of a cigarette or a bite of food to soothe my soul.

So it hurt when my friend called me out for something I hadn't been able to be honest with myself about. I grumbled on my way home, allowing my mind and emotions to gather into a small storm as I stepped into my dimly lit studio apartment sometime after midnight. I sat on my couch and brooded, or at least that's what I thought I was doing. It probably looked more like sulking. I was upset—not at my friend but at my life and the unhealthy bits of myself he had forced me to look at.

I picked up my phone and opened an app I knew all too well. With a few quick swipes, I ordered a whole pizza and some dessert. I deserved it. I was sad. Or so I told myself. After another half hour of sulking, I realized my late-night junk food hadn't arrived. I looked down when my phone started buzzing. It was my friend. I rolled my eyes and picked up.

"Hello?"

"Hey, Nathan, did you order a pizza and dessert?"

What? How did he know? My stomach dropped. I had just gotten mad at him, told him off, and assured myself I had my health under control. This wasn't good.

"Well, I guess your app thought you were still at my house and delivered it to me."

I was flooded with shame, and I could feel the red in my cheeks. My unhealthy ways were thrust into the light. Talk about quick accountability. I wasn't too ashamed to get the pizza and pastries and eat them, but the next morning I decided things had to change.

Health is a tricky thing, and out of all the subjects in this book, this is the one I feel least excited to address. Not because it's not important but because it's one I struggle with. And one I want to believe isn't that important.

Often in religious circles, physical health takes a back seat to spiritual practices. We put almost all the emphasis on heart and mind, while often completely ignoring the thing that holds them. This way of thinking fails to realize the very real connection both our hearts and our minds have to our bodies—the bodies God created for us to use for Him.

Perhaps this is a reaction to the opposite and equally extreme and incorrect thinking that our bodies are everything. Modern culture tells us we are nothing but physical beings. Hollywood constantly barrages us with billboards, magazine covers, and sexy movies that place ultimate value on youth, strength, and sex appeal. But what if both these visions for human physicality are wrong? What if we were never supposed to ignore physical health *or* worship it? What if there's a different way of thinking that tells us what our bodies and souls were made for and how we ought to value the flesh God has crafted for us?

God says we are made in His image. He did not make a mistake by giving us bodies. Actually, He revels in them. In the Old Testament, we see laid out the time and care God took in creating the bodies of Adam and Eve and the strict guidelines for what to put into them. We see Paul compare our spiritual lives to athletes in a positive way. And we see the God who created everything entering a body and living among us to carry out world-changing acts. Scripture is not ambiguous about the value of what it often refers to as the temples that house our very souls.

Bodies are important. They allow us to interact with the created world around us. When we don't value our physical health, we don't value the call God has on our lives or take seriously the mission He has laid before us.

Part of becoming a good man is learning how to responsibly care for the body God has given us, a body that was made for a purpose. It can be hard when culture encourages us to indulge in behaviors that are detrimental to our bodies, whether it's porn, fast food, hookups, smoking, or heavy drinking. We've made habits of the unhealthy, and we've dug ourselves into a pit. All the while, we are continually confronted with images of utter perfection in every superhero and men's magazine. Climbing out of the pit can feel like a task too daunting to attempt, which causes us to linger in a cycle of unhealth. Though we know that physical health is important, living the life of health we desire feels both unrealistic and out of reach.

When I was fifty pounds overweight and out of breath every time I walked up a flight of stairs, it was hard for me to even look at what it would take to become healthy. I simply didn't want to face myself.

I didn't realize that ignoring my physical well-being was detrimentally affecting my mental and spiritual health. Each time I saw the disappointing figure in the mirror, I found myself less confident, less happy, less focused, and less able to make healthy choices in all areas of my life.

To cope, I turned to the very same bad habits that had brought me there in the first place. I was bingeing on comfort food late at night, staying on my couch to avoid engaging with the world, and separating myself from the people and community I so desperately needed.

For better or worse, our bodies, hearts, and minds are linked, and one area of unhealth affects all the others. If you ignore your physical health, it will adversely affect your spiritual and mental health. What do we do? How do we begin to take care of our bodies when we feel so far from where we should be? How do we focus on our health without turning it into an idol?

Because we live in a sedentary age, it takes intention and dedication to be healthy. But perhaps it doesn't have to be a chore. We were created for a purpose—one that originally enabled us to work and create, as well as explore and enjoy the world and the people around us. In the old days, when people lived off the land, they worked with their hands, putting in long, hard hours. They used their bodies.

To begin the journey to health, we must look at the process not as one of ultimate pain but as a chance to explore how to live more fully. Many of us spend our days at a desk, a cubicle, or—if you're a writer or actor waiting for his next role like me—a couch. Finding health doesn't come as easily now that we aren't living in an age that naturally requires us to use our bodies for survival. While I struggle often with investing in my physical health, whenever I make the choice to invest, I find that all of me benefits. Spending a few hours a week or several moments a day doing something active and healthy for my body better enables both my mind and my heart to work unencumbered.

There have been moments in my life, after months and sometimes years of bodily neglect, that I am suddenly forced to recognize the effect living in such a way has had on me. And when I let that realization sink in, I find the motivation to take care of my body, because it means I am also taking care of my soul.

I've always loved venturing into the wild, so whenever I get the chance, I jump at the opportunity to take a hike, especially in my hometown in the mountains of Colorado. But even when I'm not there, I have an affinity for exploring the cities I live in and travel to. A few times a week, after a long day of sitting in front of a screen, I make myself get up and go for a walk. It's not always easy or comfortable, but afterward I'm always glad I went.

Embracing health can mean finding the things (perhaps new things) you love to do physically and committing to doing them. Maybe you enjoy exploring a city or the wilderness, or perhaps you need to get some aggression out and want to take up boxing. Maybe you are happiest taking a dance class or preparing for a Tough Mudder (an endurance event in which participants complete ten- to twelve-mile-long obstacle courses) or playing Ultimate Frisbee or shooting hoops with friends. Maybe just going to the gym and learning some basic workout routines is best. Or maybe, for some of us, embracing health means being willing to give something up—smoking, fast food, soda, beer, or TV.

Health is not a line we cross but a direction we constantly travel. One that will affect not only your body but also your mind and soul. Ultimately, it's a direction that will take each of us closer to the good men we were created to be.

Questions for Reflection

1. Do you think your physical health affects your mental and spiritual health?

2. What's the hardest part for you when it comes to making healthy choices?

3. What are three ways you can begin to implement healthy physical activity into your daily life?

> Don't you realize that in a race everyone runs, but only one person gets the prize? So run to win! All athletes are disciplined in their training. They do it to win a prize that will fade away, but we do it for an eternal prize. So I run with purpose in every step. I am not just shadowboxing. I discipline my body like an athlete, training it to do what it should. Otherwise, I fear that after preaching to others I myself might be disqualified.
>
> 1 Corinthians 9:24–27

A PRAYER FOR
OUR BODIES

God, maker of our hearts, minds, and bodies,
we pray that we might honor You with the
vessel You have given us to inhabit.

You have designed us with beautiful purpose and
intention. Help us do what is necessary to pursue health
so we may better live out the story You have written for
us and more fully enjoy the world You have created.

Help us in our journey toward health in every
area of our lives. Give us strength to press on,
grace when we fall short, and wisdom to live
the way You have intended us to live.

Amen.

SEVEN

Emotional

Perhaps our eyes need to be washed by our tears once in a while so we can see life with a clearer view again.

Unknown

I sat staring at the walls of my empty apartment. I could feel a ball of anxiety, anger, frustration, and hurt churning in my gut.

I pushed it down.

The space around me was covered with remnants of her: an old sweatshirt, a picture, CDs. Each item seemed to stare at me, telling me I had failed, reminding me of what I'd lost, prodding a deep sadness I could feel in my chest.

I pushed it down.

Out my window I saw the sun sink behind the shadowy Los Angeles hills, serving as a metaphor for my emotional state, unearthing the depression I had been trying with all my might to keep at bay.

I pushed it down.

I had been pushing it down for months as I watched my relationship with the person I had committed to spending the rest of my life with disintegrate after five years. I thought that maybe if I could just stay strong, keep a stiff upper lip, and be good enough, I could save us. Perhaps it was my English blood that kept me setting my brow, believing different variations of "keep strong and carry on," and assuring myself I could make this right if I was strong enough.

But I didn't feel strong. In fact, I felt tired and weak as I sat in my empty apartment for hours with only my thoughts keeping me company. The occasional checkup phone calls from friends and family left me weary, and it was getting more difficult to keep the emotions at bay.

One night I decided that I needed some fresh air. I stepped outside into the dry evening smog and began walking to my car. I didn't really have a plan, but I got in and started driving, windows down and music blaring, toward the Americana movie theater. *Yeah, that's it*, I told myself. *I'll see a movie. Maybe that'll get my mind off these pesky emotions I've been fighting.*

With popcorn and candy in hand, I took my seat. I had avoided anything too heavy. No dramas that might tap at the fragile walls I had been building around my soul. Instead, I had decided on a new digital animated kids' movie. *Perfect*, I told myself, *only mindless escapism here.*

As I was settling in, I noticed I was surrounded by hundreds of moms and kids—what a funny sight I must've been: a six-foot-three grown man sitting among so many women and children. But the mom on the other side of me smiled at me and told me how much I would enjoy the flick, so I didn't worry too much about it.

The movie started, and for a while I happily escaped into the bright colors, childish humor, and wacky characters. It took place inside of a young girl's mind, where her emotions were personified by unique and engaging characters. I enjoyed the respite from the emotional war I had been waging. But then came the final scene in which the characters Grief and Joy discovered the only way to save the day was to embrace each other and face the painful reality of life together. Suddenly I felt a lump rise from my chest to my throat.

I tried to push it down.

But as the music swelled and the story unfolded, I was no longer strong enough to win this fight.

Not here, not now, I whispered in my mind. But it was too late. The tears had finally broken through my determined eyes and were running down my face.

I cried, and this time no amount of manly stoicism could stand against the current of emotion I had been running from all those months. I was finally set free from all the emotions that had held me captive for so long. I turned to the mom sitting next to me, who also had tears running down her face, and we meekly smiled at each other. I had finally given in and let the healing work of emotion take over.

As I left the theater that night, I felt new and fresh, like the balloon I had held in my chest had finally popped. I could finally breathe. The sadness was still there. I was still going home to an empty apartment and an ambiguous future. But by letting go of the control I had so vehemently held on to for months, I knew I could keep moving forward, that healing waited for me.

"Real men don't cry."

Like I mentioned briefly at the beginning of the book, I'm sure many of us have heard this sentiment in one form or another from a very young age. Maybe we heard it from our dads, brothers, or friends. Perhaps we heard it when we skinned our knees and others pressured us to keep the tears at bay so as not to embarrass ourselves and let our pain be known in front of our peers. Perhaps we heard it when we were a little older and got our heart broken for the first time. Every time, this insidious phrase wrapped around our throat like a vice, threatening us with labels we feared to own, such as "weak."

Even now we repeat these words to ourselves as they echo in our heart and mind. When our world comes crashing down around us, we believe that real men don't feel or show emotion or cry—but by now we have become experts at hiding those painful emotions, we have spent years pushing down and suppressing these "weak" displays of feeling. But like anything in life, the emotion, pain, and hurt don't disappear; they simply lie dormant in our souls and hearts.

These other common tropes are also handed to us as boys: "Man up," "Crying is for girls," "Stop being so emotional." No matter the specific words, they all serve one purpose, which is to pressure us into telling the world we are okay when inside we are not. We don't hear the truth that it's okay to not be okay. But these words that ring in so many of our minds have deeply affected our psyches and our ability to healthily process the deep emotions *everyone* feels. Eventually we don't even know how to truly experience the very real emotions we were created to feel.

At their core, emotions are indicators of our heart's condition. If we ignore them, like symptoms of a sickness, we only harm ourselves, allowing the cancer of a broken soul to eat away at us from the inside. It's hard not to allow this to happen when we are taught to deal with our pain by pushing it down and stuffing it inside so we're not viewed as helpless. In reality, we are helpless, just like every other human to walk this earth. But we continue to repress our emotions for the sake of pride, to protect our egos. We do it for safety so we won't have to deal with the discomfort of our pain. And we do it because we think it's what we're supposed to do to keep our world from falling apart.

When we stuff our emotions, the pressure will grow and grow until we finally burst. Some men push their feelings down only to have those repressed emotions bubble up and burst, resulting in abuse, violence, and even self-harm and suicide. The ability to work through and face our emotions is literally an issue of life and death.

Not letting our emotions take over and not giving in to our weaknesses can seem like okay things on the surface. There is good to be found in being resilient and resolute. I mean, who wants to be known as the weepy guy who can't take a punch? But at the end of the day, we're humans with emotions we were created to work through and feel rather than escape from.

I deal with the temptation to run from my emotions almost every day, because they are often painful and uncomfortable. They make me feel vulnerable, weak, small, and even fearful, when I so want to be untouchable, strong, big, and impervious. But the older I get and the more life humbles me, I realize emotions don't hold me back from who I was created to be; they move me forward to become the better man God created me to be.

The shortest verse in the entire Bible is, to me, perhaps the most powerful.

"Jesus wept" (John 11:35 NIV).

One of Jesus's closest friends, Lazarus, had died while He was away. Upon His return, Jesus was confronted with the news. Jesus, the all-powerful God of all creation in human form, didn't put on a stoic face and "fix" things; instead, He dropped to His knees and cried. Jesus took the space and time to feel sadness deeply, to let His followers and close friends see His grief, and to grieve with them.

And just a little while later, Jesus brought His friend Lazarus back to life. But still He wept. Because He knew that fully feeling His emotions was a deeply important part of being human. And when He wept, it didn't weaken Him. It was the necessary process for healing and new life to take place.

I recently finished watching a TV show with a friend. Because we are poor, starving artists who can't go out like the cool kids, we needed something to binge watch, and the series we picked looked like a fun thriller.

There's a running joke in the show where someone calls the secret agent in the middle of a mission as he's dodging bullets and running from explosions and asks how he's doing, to which the secret agent pauses for one second before replying, "Pretty good." But as the scenario repeats, it becomes heavier and heavier, until you finally realize the secret agent is saying "pretty good" because he knows that's all he can say.

In the final episode, when this agent has given up everything he loves, has bullet holes in his body, has lost his best friend and been betrayed by his love, he receives a call from his handler who, ignorant of his current situation, asks, "How are you?" The agent, covered in blood and on the brink of death, replies as a tear runs down his face, "Pretty good."

What I didn't expect at the end of this adventure show was to have a tear rolling down my cheek because I, on my couch in my workout shorts, could see myself in the main character and felt so understood. No, I don't have blood covering my body. I haven't lost my best friend, and I haven't dodged any bullets. But I bear the heavy weight of a broken world. All too often when someone asks me how I am, I can feel myself pushing down all the painful emotions, gulping the tears that have been at bay for years, and doing what I can not to break. I often reply, "Pretty good."

But maybe for the sake of ourselves and the world, we can't say this any longer. Maybe we need to let ourselves feel and, as scary as it is, let ourselves break so that we can be put back together.

The thing is, our emotions will come out sooner or later whether we like it or not. We can try to keep them in, we can try to hold them down, but they will come out. And when we don't face and process them in healthy and healing ways, they will find a more destructive way out. One that almost always harms either ourselves or others.

When we regularly suppress the painful emotions, we end up suppressing all our emotions—we push down the good with the painful and cut ourselves off from experiencing life's beautiful moments. For the survival of our souls, we need to find a safe place where we can fall apart. This place will be different for each of us. Perhaps it's in the presence of a therapist, pastor, family member, or friend. It's important to find ways to fully feel, cry, and express your real, powerful emotions and pain.

Though we live in a painful world in which we must process the emotions that arise out of brokenness, it's also a wonderful world that invites us to feel deeply the beautiful moments of life too. To laugh loudly at an inside joke, to stand in awe of a starry sky over a roaring sea, to passionately sing our favorite song, and even to cry sweet tears during a touching moment.

We need at all costs to release this harmful idea that real men don't cry. It's tired, it's worn out, it's regressive, it's wrong, and it's dangerous. It's not easy to let go of deeply ingrained ideas about how men are supposed to deal with pain and heartache, but to be truly good men, we need to learn to become tender. We need to start tearing down the walls we've built around our hearts and minds and more fully embrace the beauty and strength that come with honesty. We do this by authentically showing up and working through our feelings.

By revealing our vulnerability in safe places, we open ourselves up to empathy, love, grace, and healing—all things we can then offer to others who do the same.

———————

Facing our emotions isn't an easy thing we can learn to do overnight. Men have been struggling with this for thousands of years. I still have an anxiety attack when I look at a new script and see I have to cry for a scene. Some of my peers find it's easy to tap into their feelings in order to realistically portray the heavy emotions of crying, but I find it hard to do. During those kinds of scenes, I have to unlearn in a matter of moments the skills I've acquired through the years that help me push down my emotions. Instead, I must allow them to come up and be seen and felt. It's challenging but necessary and worthwhile. And when we begin this process, we will see how wonderful it is to feel things, how it moves us forward, and how it adds to, rather than detracts from, our strength.

Next time you watch a touching movie; see a beautiful night sky covered with stars; listen to a meaningful song; or go through a breakup, a move, or a death, when you feel a tear in the corner of your eye or a lump in your throat, don't push it down. Your body and your heart are working together to help you through. Let it free and feel the strength and relief that come from fully experiencing the emotions you were created to feel. The experience will bring strength, healing, and peace.

So perhaps the world will carry on the lie that real men don't cry, but I can assure you, good men do.

Questions for Reflection

1. Do you view men who show their emotions and cry as weak or strong?
2. Do you have a hard time expressing or showing your emotions? Why or why not?
3. How can you learn to work through your emotions rather than stuff them down?

Jesus wept.

John 11:35 NIV

THE EMOTIONAL

God, the Creator of our bodies and souls, our
thoughts and emotions, help us learn to feel
fully what You have designed us to feel.

Jesus said blessed are those who mourn, for
they will be comforted by You. And we want
connection with You, so let us not run away from
our feelings but learn to let them lead us to You.

Teach us that true strength involves vulnerability. We don't
need to escape from the sadness and brokenness of the
world but to use them to better know You and ourselves.

As we face our deep and dark emotions, please
be present in them, heal us from the hurt, and
give us wisdom to help others do the same.

Walk with us through our lament, speak
to us in our sadness, meet with us in our
mourning, and lead us to new life.

Amen.

EIGHT

Authentic

A ragamuffin knows he's only a beggar at the door of God's mercy.

Brennan Manning

Like a whitewashed house where the cracks in the wood are deliberately covered or a blemished stage actor with carefully placed makeup, sometimes it seems that there are two parts of me, like I am split into two separate selves. One that people see and one that very few know.

The first is my outer self, the one many people know and recognize, the one I present to the world at church and social functions and share on social media.

The second part is my inner self, the hidden part, the one very few people see. I have learned to skillfully conceal it behind my outer self, and within its shadows are the more broken, human, and real bits of who I am.

I do this to keep safe from judgmental eyes and because it's more comfortable not having to face my broken places. I do this out of the hope that if I look good enough, maybe I will be good enough. But perhaps, really, I do this out of fear. The fear that if the entirety of myself—scars, warts, blemishes, and all—were on display before the world, I wouldn't be fully loved or wanted. But in this journey of chasing after my Creator, I've learned little by little that hiding and covering my true self doesn't keep me safe at all—it keeps me from freedom.

Sometimes when I feel that I am fractured, splitting into these two parts, I watch a video.

It's a video of a barefoot man in ripped jeans sitting behind a church piano. He's speaking to a crowd, exposing his dark mistakes, fears, doubts, and failures. He goes on to play a song he wrote. It's a prayer to God, with deep and raw words wrapped in a delicate piano melody. The singer's prayer, his song, and his cry acknowledge both his frailty and God's presence.

I feel less alone when I watch it. When the artist looks at his fragility and asks God for strength, I find I can do so also.

The man in the video is Rich Mullins. Rich was a poet, prophet, and musician in the eighties and nineties. He wrote some of the most popular praise songs we still sing today—like "Awesome God" and "Sing Your Praise to the Lord"—that many associate with tidy, pristine religion. But the man behind those songs was anything but tidy and pristine.[1]

Rich was a broken human, but this wasn't something he hid. Instead, it was something he was very honest about in an effort to point to his Creator and the greatness of how God works with and loves us despite our limitations. Rich struggled with addiction, both sexual and substance, and he cursed like a sailor. He was prone to outbursts of anger, especially when music labels would ask him to write another "hit" when his raw, unfiltered lyrics about his doubts and failures caused declining sales and discomfort within the Christian market.

Despite being a popular musician with plenty of money coming in, he was often homeless—he slept on friends' couches and asked his accountant to provide him with only a small allowance so he could give the rest away. Rich's concerts were often in churches filled with Bible-thumping, suit-wearing Christians. He was usually barefoot in tattered jeans, and he often upset attendees with his uncensored words.

In the video, Rich speaks candidly about a time when he was in a hotel room in Europe on tour, unable to sleep, fighting the urge to watch porn on the TV. I can only imagine the discomfort the conservative audience felt as this ragamuffin was talking about the more real parts of himself, parts we all have, on a stage reserved for righteous sermons. The song he goes on to play is called "Hold Me Jesus," and it reveals that Rich deeply recognized his need for God.

Rich wrote, sang, and lived in a way that I want to live—authentically, hiding nothing, and baring all in the hopes that through honesty and childlike dependence on God he would find what he was looking for, what we are all looking for.

He lived this way until the day he tragically died in a car accident on his way to a concert. Rich called himself a ragamuffin not because he hated who he was but because authenticity was more important to him than presenting a polished façade, and he knew it was the only way he could stand honest before God.

That authenticity has gone on to inspire many people to connect all their human pieces and integrate their real selves into the whole but fractured person God made them, not hiding who they are but striving to be transparent about the human experience. Authenticity like Rich's is scary, but I think perhaps it leads to freedom. I see that freedom in Rich's life, and it's something I crave too.

———

Authenticity is a buzzword we hear often, sometimes from the lips of popular internet "influencers" and sometimes on fast-food ads, but authenticity at its core is the unhidden and blatant truth of something or, more specifically, someone. Authenticity is a human desire, something we all crave in our lives, perhaps now more than ever because there's seemingly so little of it left. We are confronted with a new cultural norm where photoshopped photos, perfectly manicured social media feeds, and slick advertising are typical, creating an unattainable standard of perfection. It leaves many of us feeling like we have to hide the less than "post-worthy" parts of ourselves.

And it's easy to hide those parts of ourselves now. It's simple—and far more comfortable—for me to share only photos displaying my best angles. And while I do have good angles, both inside and out, like everyone else I also have less-than-flattering angles. As we begin to hide those parts of ourselves, it becomes easier to believe they don't exist in one another, that we're the only ones who are concealing something. But then we come across someone like Rich, a beautiful and talented man who also had deeply broken and human places, both of which he showed. He didn't fear what others thought; he stood in freedom before the world and God.

Hiding is natural, and I'm certainly not saying we ought to show and expose all of ourselves (physically or emotionally) to everyone. There is wisdom in knowing what to keep sacred and safely away from those we cannot trust with our whole selves.

But we must have someone in our lives with whom we are free to be completely honest about the *whole* of who we are. Maybe that's a family member, a counselor, or a friend, but until we are fully known, we won't believe it's possible to be fully loved, and this will affect our relationship with God and others.

There's another guy I admire—someone on social media who I want to be.

His feed is filled with perfectly posed images of his meaningful life and beautiful wife and kids.

He's a successful author and speaker who gets tens of thousands of likes and endless comments about how wonderful he is.

He's invited to speak at all the cool places, and he hangs out with all the cool people.

He's fit, successful, and popular, and he even owns a Pinterest-worthy home.

And every time I scroll by his photo or click on his profile, I am filled with a depressing realization of what I don't have and what I am not.

I want what he has.

I don't have the perfect relationship and family I thought I was guaranteed by now. Instead, I have a past of heartbreak. I don't own a chic home. Instead, I travel many months of the year, living on friends' couches or in tiny studio apartments in old buildings with barely enough room to stand up. I don't have the picture-perfect body I want. Instead, I have struggled with my weight. I often avoid the mirror because it seems to point out all the flaws of my imperfect shell. I am not a spiritual leader and picture of morality. More often than not, I find that my times with God are filled with confessions of things I should've conquered years ago or frustration about the circumstances He has given me. I have never been a *New York Times* bestselling author and don't get invited to speak at many cool events, with the cool people. I watch a lot of Netflix and often hang out with the same five people. I'm not rich. Instead, I have often wondered if buying groceries would overdraw my account.

I want what the Instagram guy has, and because I don't have it, I have felt both disappointment in myself and bitterness toward not only him but also God.

As I was talking this through with my therapist, Jeff, he encouraged me to look past this guy's pictures. He asked me if I truly believed his life was picture-perfect, with no problems, insecurities, or regrets. Immediately, I knew the answer to that question. Of course he didn't have a perfect life. Not because I knew some secret about him, but because I know that life is hard and people are broken, no matter how their Instagram feed might appear. I knew his life wasn't all that I had made it to be, because every one of us is affected by living in a broken world.

Most of us have a guy like this in our lives. Maybe it's someone you know—a friend, a brother, or even (dare I say it) a pastor.

But whoever they are, these guys are still just humans. So often when we look at them, we see what appears to be a flawless life in comparison to our inconsistent, messy reality. It can cause us to grow bitter and hide our own humanity for fear of not measuring up. But the reality is, no matter how good someone looks, we all taste the bitter twinge of a real and broken world. We're all affected no matter how polished our outside persona may look.

Far too often we hear the devastating news that another successful star or well-loved leader has died by suicide. And sometimes it hits even closer to home, when someone we know and cherish, someone who loves God, loses the battle that many of us had no idea was raging inside of them.

It has been found that comedians have some of the highest rates of depression of all artists.[2] At first that seems strangely and sadly ironic. But at second glance, I see perhaps why that is. Comedians' very job is to make others laugh and smile and to make palatable the difficult truths of this world—perhaps dull the sharp sting of reality into something we can laugh at for an hour.

But, really, we all do the same thing when we show the world only our best selves. We use jokes, jobs, or social media captions to lighten, hide, and disguise the very real and deep pain we feel. And the sad thing is, choosing to escape from this reality and hide our true selves hurts not only us but others too. It isolates us and causes loneliness, as we think we are the only ones who aren't picture-perfect.

But then someone like Rich comes along and bravely reveals not only the beautiful but also the broken parts of humanity. They reach into our hearts and remind us that we're not alone.

———————

How many times have we heard the trope about men not asking for directions for fear of looking incompetent? The reality is, we all are lost in one way or another and we all need directions, both in our cars and in our lives.

One of our biggest hurdles is embracing authenticity. We have voices in our minds that tell us that real men don't have weaknesses, problems, or brokenness. And if they do, they don't talk about or acknowledge it. They figure things out on their own. Keep calm and carry on!

The reality is, every man you know is scared, insecure, and human. We must go beyond the façade culture presents—the movies stars, magazine covers, and social media figures that leave us feeling like we need to look strong and put together all the time, that we are the only ones struggling, and that we must hide parts of who we really are. If we are to be *truly* strong, healthy, integrated, and connected men, we must begin by being honest about who we are—*all* of who we are—and look at ourselves not with shame but grace, the same grace we extend to others. The same grace God offers all of us, knowing how much we need it. The grace we receive only when we are brave enough to acknowledge we need it.

Questions for Reflection

1. What effect do you think this inauthentic world has on us?
2. Do you feel the need to hide parts of yourself? If so, which ones?
3. Who do you find yourself envious of and why?

> When you pray, don't be like the hypocrites who love to pray publicly on street corners and in the synagogues where everyone can see them. I tell you the truth, that is all the reward they will ever get. But when you pray, go away by yourself, shut the door behind you, and pray to your Father in private. Then your Father, who sees everything, will reward you.
>
> Matthew 6:5–6

THE AUTHENTIC

O God, I acknowledge You are the One who
knows my innermost being, the One who created
me, and the One who knows me inside and out.
It is You alone who knows my motivations,
dreams, thoughts, fears, and feelings.
From You I can hide no part of myself.

Thank You that while knowing me fully You love me
fully, and because of Your great love I do not need
to hide. I can be honest with myself, others, and most
important, You about who I really am. It is then that I
can begin to discover who You created me to be.

I pray that You would help me live an authentic life
and not hide behind the masks I am so accustomed
to, knowing my acceptance, freedom, forgiveness,
and identity have already been spoken by You.

Amen.

Good Man // A Poem

What is a good man?
I really want to know.
I've been searching and searching and got nothing
    to show.

What were we made for?
Why are we here?
It's got to be more
Than just how we appear.

Even if it is,
We're not doing that great.
Men today have become
Angry and given in to their hate.

We've become selfish
And we take what we please.
"Don't think of the consequences,
That's for the weak."

We curse the wind
And feed our pride.

Completely ignoring
The cancer inside.

We don't need any help
And won't confess our sins.
"Real men don't cry
Or let anyone in."

Then some of us are just lost,
Looking for home.
But our dark is too thick,
And we walk all alone.

But I need to believe
That there's got to be more.
'Cause if God created us,
There's something He created us for.

Maybe we were made to be whole,
Honest, and true.
To protect all that's beautiful
And to see our work through.

To love with abandon
And own our own scars.
To see real redemption
Take place in our hearts.

To laugh at the future
And embrace all we can.
To know our Savior.
Maybe that's a good man.

So what is a good man?
Maybe it's this:
One who lets his Creator
Tell him who he is.

NINE

Romantic

You don't have sex with a body, you have sex with a soul.

Jefferson Bethke

I held my breath for just a few seconds to make sure I was completely alone in the house. The family was off running errands and I sat in my room, door closed, looking at the bookshelf next to my old bunk bed. On any other normal afternoon, I would have grabbed a comic book and pored over the pictures, but that day I went to grab something even more exciting. My teen study Bible.

A friend had recently told me there was a secret and even sordid collection of pages I had seemingly overlooked: Song of Solomon. I opened the book, skipping past Psalms and Proverbs, and headed toward what suddenly felt like a forbidden book. As I read, my young mind missing 90 percent of the sensual imagery, I felt something in my body ignite as I read the word *breast*. There it was, written right in front of my eyes in the Bible I had been carrying around all these years.

This part of the Bible had never been talked about in Sunday school, and I immediately knew why. It was exciting and it felt a little wrong, but I didn't stop reading and rereading the image-inducing words until I heard the front door open as my family arrived home from their errands. I quickly closed the Good Book, a bit intoxicated from this new feeling. I wasn't quite sure what to make of this poem about sex, but something about those words excited and intrigued me in a way that nothing else in the Bible had. I didn't know what it was, but I knew it was powerful.

It wasn't long after reading Song of Solomon that I found myself again experiencing the same nervous but powerful physical and mental excitement as I sat in my dark room lit only by the light of my computer screen, clicking through pictures of naked women. But this time when I was done, something else was attached to the intoxicating feeling—shame.

I knew I was doing something wrong; I knew those bodies weren't mine to look at. But there was something so alluring about the feeling I got, a feeling that called me back over and over again. It was then that I began a lifelong struggle between something I so desire and doing what I know to be right.

I have liked girls for as long as I can remember. Everything about them—the way they smell and laugh at my jokes, the way their eyes look shimmering in the sun, and their skin in the night. I love their voices and the feel of their hands on my arm. I love that they think differently than I do and that their minds, emotions, and bodies are wholly other than mine.

I remember at seven years old playing on a playground at church one afternoon when I began running after a girl named Kelsey. I started chasing girls that day and I haven't stopped.

I grew up watching old black-and-white movies with my mom, the kind that would come on the AMC channel. They had dashing men in suits and beautiful women in flowing dresses who were caught up in classy romance stories. Transatlantic accents flowed through the scratchy speakers as the overly acted scenes played out with characters dramatically exclaiming things like "It was always you," "I've loved you for so long," or "You're the only one my eyes could ever see."

Perhaps these movies are silly or old-fashioned, but they created a picture for me of what love and romance could look like—a dance both careful and bold, subtle and beautiful. These old movies could be hyperbolic, but even today when I flip by the AMC channel, I'll occasionally stop and watch for a minute. I enjoy the tension and romance (yes, guys can like chick flicks). I love watching the story unfold as the handsome protagonist, with determination and unstoppable affection, pursues the woman.

As I sit here writing, I can recall the black-and-white scene in which a man with slicked back hair and a tie tenderly but strongly takes hold of his lover and kisses her beneath the stars, one of her legs rising as she falls into his embrace.

———

Being a pastor's kid and growing up inside the walls of the church, I was confronted by an unhealthy and reactionary perspective about the human sex drive. Religion has often been associated with the suppression of our natural curiosity about sex. I've heard about movements telling women to cover their

entire bodies out of fear that men will look at them inappropri-
ately. I've heard youth pastors hand out arbitrary dating rules,
like never be alone with someone of the opposite sex past nine
o'clock at night or for more than an hour. There are also more
extreme examples, like men shouldn't touch (hold hands, hug,
kiss) a woman until they are married—and even then, be careful. This strikes me as both missing the point and encouraging
fear about something God created to be beautiful.

But then having lived and worked in Hollywood off and on
for the past ten years, I'm exposed daily to the other side of the
spectrum. As I drive down Sunset Boulevard, I'm confronted
with countless billboards exploiting the bodies of women for
money or watching men proposition, sexually harass, and objectify women—even ones I know and love. And I'm sadly not
surprised at all by the recent headlines in the news about the
#MeToo movement. Women are sharing their abhorrent expe-
riences of men in powerful positions who have wielded their
influence to harass, abuse, and assault them.

Some people react to the natural and powerful sex drive of
humans with complete denial and suppression, attempting to
quell our God-given inclinations toward the opposite sex. But
to many, sex isn't a big deal. Mainstream culture tells us we can
do what we want and treats sex as something casual and in-
consequential when it should be treated as something sacred.

Both are destructive views on sex and romance. And both
seem to completely miss the nuanced but important design God
created in each of us.

I remember when I was twenty years old, just having arrived
in the big city to follow my dreams. I was heading to a church

on the hill for a young adults group. That night I fell in love with one of the worship band singers. She had greeted me at the door and when I saw her smile, my usual fast-talking confidence disappeared into a jumble of awkward words and pocketed hands. After I joined the worship team (with sincere motives, of course), she asked for my number and I began to drive her to practice each week. We built a friendship that eventually blossomed into a romance.

This woman, wholly other than me, would spend the next six years of her life with me. In that time I learned to love this person I had been immediately attracted to. She wasn't just another picture on a screen but a woman with hopes, dreams, fears, and insecurities. I cared deeply for who she was—her heart, her mind, her soul. Eventually we made vows and were married.

Sadly, after a year of being wed to this woman I had fallen so deeply in love with, our marriage ended and she walked away from me. I was heartbroken and didn't know if I would ever be fixed. I moved from LA to NYC shortly after the separation to escape the lingering ghosts of memories hiding behind every corner. I was talking to a friend and told him I finally knew why people settled for one-night stands. It sounded easier than involving your heart in something that might break it. You're able to satisfy your skin-deep desires without having to suffer the potential emotional destruction that comes from connecting your soul with another person.

I soon found myself struggling yet again, answering the echoing loneliness and hurt with pictures on a screen. But every time I shut off my computer, I felt even worse than I had before. Because the desire of my heart, the desire for connection, was deeper than just sexual pleasure. It was for true and authentic connection in a romantic and intimate way—to be bare both in body and soul with someone who would love me as I loved her. No matter how many pictures I tried to distract myself with, they couldn't stand up to the beauty of living out the design for sex and connection God created—one I had experienced and lost.

Years later, as I read over the Song of Solomon, I find its power is still there. I understand it perhaps a bit better and no longer fear being caught reading the word *breast*, but inside the flowing poem is a deep beauty coming from a man's longing for a woman and his pursuit of her. It describes with poetic prose the passion, sexuality, and romance—the relational dance that is the powerful attraction of souls and bodies longing for connection with each other. Song of Solomon harkens back to the first story of Genesis, where God created man and in seeing he was incomplete, created woman from man's rib. He created them for each other, endowing each with a powerful desire to connect and experience becoming one.

But something happened after the first chapter of Genesis. Something went terribly wrong. When Adam and Eve ate of the forbidden fruit, they recognized their nakedness and found a rift in the beautiful connection they had shared. That rift between men and women continues today, as we are constantly confronted by divorce, assault, sexism, bitterness, heartbreak, objectification, sexual trafficking, and an ever-unraveling list of destructive behaviors and actions revolving around gender and sexuality.

I wish I could say at almost thirty years old that I finally have this whole sex and relationship thing figured out. I wish I could say I don't struggle at all, that the temptation to be flippant with my sexuality no longer holds power over me. I wish I could say I have matured past youthful mistakes and I live and act perfectly in step with how a good man ought to when it comes to women, sexuality, and relationships, but that is simply not true. I still struggle with lust outside of relationships and sexual boundaries within them. I fight a mental world of fantasy, laugh at jokes I know are wrong, and idolize relationships with women. At times I've found myself actively pursuing women more than I do God.

There is a beauty in the design of romantic relationship, attraction, and sexuality, but like everything beautiful God has created, we are capable of misusing what was made to be a blessing in our lives and turning it into a curse.

I think about God's design in contrast to our modern picture of sexuality and love (if you can call it that). I see it played out in the movies where women are objectified as sex objects and men are reduced to cavemen whose sole focus is adding as many notches to their bedpost as possible. I see how, in real life, lonely men have stopped trying to win women's affection and instead have turned to the quick, cheap, and destructive habit of typing in a search bar unspeakably depraved things for an easy and sad release.

I see the poor condition of relationships and how our everyday romantic practices have fallen so far from the deep, passionate displays of love we read in poetry and classic books and been reduced to opening an app and typing, "You up?" We allow ourselves to engage in cheap encounters that leave us feeling even more empty and alone. This is not how we were made to find love.

I miss the good ole days, when men valued and protected women instead of preying on and using them. The days when romance was meaningful and indicated true affection, not just a quick, loveless rendezvous that leaves both people hurt and even more alone.

Whether we like it or not, love, affection, sex, relationships, and romance are intrinsic to the human condition. Both beautiful and sacred, they are meant to be lived out with care and thought. But in our loneliness and hunger for affection, we have settled for and bought into imitations of God's creation. Ultimately, when we try to fill the desires God gives us outside of His design for a true, deep, sacrificial, and committed love, we will find little else but brokenness.

Sexual intimacy, romantic connection, and relationships are weighty and meaningful parts of life. In the correct context, they're life-giving. But because they're powerful, they must be treated as such. They're not something to be scared of and protected from, but they're also not something to handle flippantly and carelessly. Either approach can have heavy and destructive consequences.

As good men, can we return to a high view of sex and relationships? One that encourages us to engage with sex only in the way it was designed; commit to relationships even when it's hard; and value women as whole people, not to be used but to be loved. We must learn to view romantic relationships as uniting two bodies and two souls in the context of commitment, protection, and honor, not selfishly seeking only personal gain. We must learn to see sex, intimacy, and relationships as ways to better love and be loved inside a lifelong bond, not as drugs we "hit and quit" when we feel like it.

Paul suggests we treat each other like brothers and sisters, honoring and valuing each other above ourselves. I grew up with two amazingly bright, talented, and strong sisters—Sarah and Joy. And because I know what whole and beautiful people they are, the thought of anyone seeing or using them for anything less makes me righteously furious. But every woman is a sister, a mother, a daughter, a human—someone to be valued and respected. To treat women as anything less is an affront to God and humanity.

When we, as men, value women as complex and beautiful human beings (all of them, even the ones on the screens), hold a high view of sex, and learn the meaning of commitment, relational connection will again be something positive. We will move away from the hurts, scars, fears, and devastation many of us feel as a result of using sex and relationships for our own gain. We were designed to be men of romance and passion, not lazy indulgence.

———

I am currently in a committed relationship with a wonderful woman. She's beautiful, smart, fiery, talented, driven, fun, and godly. Sometimes I think about how easy it would have been for me to miss the amazing human that she is had I not learned to see her as a whole person.

Our love is a valuable investment of time, and the romance we created is a worthy pursuit. She is a body *and* a soul. And I get to deeply connect with her—an action that fulfills my heart, mind, and body (after marriage, guys). Building a relationship took a lot more time and effort than opening a dating app and looking for a one-night stand. But the value of what I get in return is so much more than what the world has reduced love and sexuality to. I have a hard time believing anyone would dare miss out on this if they knew what could actually exist.

The road to true love, real romance, and meaningful sexuality can be difficult, and there's not one man alive who hasn't struggled in some way or another with doing it right. But it's a necessary one for us as good men to walk, even if we do it imperfectly.

In fact, *no one* has done this perfectly. I struggle daily to walk the path of a good man when it comes to honoring women, living with sexual purity (both physically and mentally), and seeking healthy relationships. I often fail. You will too. No doubt you already have.

Luckily, we have God's grace, which enables us to get up and try again. No matter where you are, what you've done, or what's been done to you, get up and dust yourself off. Seek to live into the design of a good man that God has called you to, even here in the confusing but beautiful realm of sexuality, romance, and relationship.

Questions for Reflection

1. Do you believe that sexuality and romance are weighty subjects and it's important to learn to do them right? Why or why not?
2. In what ways do you struggle in your own life when it comes to these issues?
3. How can you begin growing and learning to better live into God's design for sexuality and relationships?

> Kiss me and kiss me again,
>   for your love is sweeter than wine.

How pleasing is your fragrance;
> your name is like the spreading fragrance of scented
> > oils.

No wonder all the young women love you!

Take me with you; come, let's run!
> The king has brought me into his bedroom.

Song of Solomon 1:1–4

A PRAYER FOR
THE ROMANTIC
AND PURE OF HEART

Lord, the Creator of heart and body, love
and intimacy, let us daily learn to see and
act out love as You have taught us.

Let us move past the practice of indulgent, selfish
desire that causes only pain and destruction to
ourselves and others. Help us learn the higher
way of treating those we are drawn to with a
self-sacrificial love that brings life, not death.

Teach us to cast off the counterfeit love of this world
for the love that You have created—one that seeks
not to use but to protect and support. One that seeks
not to objectify but to know and care for. One that
seeks not to avoid responsibility but to rise to its call.

Let us not be afraid of the desire for love and physical
intimacy You have woven intentionally into our bodies
and hearts, but instead learn the beautiful, life-
giving, mysterious way it was designed to be used.

We repent for the ways we have abused Your gift. We
humbly ask for Your forgiveness and the ability to use
our passion to better reflect You and Your great design.

Amen.

TEN

Wise

Any fool can know. The point is to understand.

Albert Einstein

I can remember sitting with a math tutor in a small, empty church classroom—an open textbook in front of me. The tutor was chewing gum, and as the time inched along, I could hear him chewing harder, his jaw clenching with frustration every time he tried to patiently explain simple algebra concepts to my inept fifteen-year-old self. My stomach had been gradually tying itself into knots over the course of the forty-five-minute lesson, and I could feel the all-too-familiar taste of my own disappointment and disgust with my lack of ability.

Later on in high school, I felt the angst and embarrassment of looking around during a test at the teens surrounding me, seemingly filling in the answers with ease, while I had spent the previous fifteen minutes staring at the paper in front of me as the words, shapes, and numbers appeared about as understandable as Latin or hieroglyphics.

————

I grew up in a family of intelligent people. My father is a specialist in education and theology, as well as a member of Mensa; my mother is a former high school teacher turned bestselling author and world-renowned speaker; and all my siblings have been successful in higher education at some of the most prestigious universities in the world.

Then, there's me . . .

The kid with mental illness and a host of debilitating learning disabilities, like obsessive-compulsive disorder (OCD), attention deficit disorder (ADD), oppositional defiant disorder (ODD), dyslexia (trouble reading), and more. The kid who was kicked out of multiple classes for causing trouble, cracking jokes, and simply not being able to work at the same level as the other kids. The kid who (still) has trouble reading for longer than fifteen minutes and panics when asked to read something out loud because the words begin mixing up in my mind. The guy who still struggles with basic math and rereads pages at a time because his mind wanders. The adult who never got a college degree and often feels "less than" when looking at friends, family, and colleagues and their diplomas and accomplishments.

Even in writing this book and looking over the paragraph I have just written, I am confronted with a barrage of grammatical errors and red underlined spelling mistakes (ironically, I spelled *intelligent* incorrectly at the beginning of this chapter), reminding me of my incomplete and wanting mental ability.

————

For as long as I can remember, I have fought the deeply held belief that I'm stupid. Even today at twenty-nine years old, I still feel a sharp twinge of insecurity when talking to intelligent and important people, fighting the fear that my mind is defective and I don't belong.

Yet learning is one of my highest and most valued priorities.

Maybe you don't deal with the exact same insecurities and conditions as I do, but I've met very few men who haven't dealt with something, perhaps imposter syndrome or a lack of ability, in one way or another. The average American reads less than one book a year,[1] and if you watch even five minutes of Jimmy Kimmel man-on-the-street interviews, you will quickly see that ignorance is widespread and a very common aspect of this generation.[2]

Ironically, we live in the information age, with every bit of knowledge the world has ever known at our fingertips. I rarely have a conversation with friends when someone doesn't pull out a smartphone to fact-check something. But because we have this information so readily available, I wonder if we have become immune to the importance of gaining information, choosing to instead spend the majority of our free time watching mindless reality TV shows, hours of inane YouTube videos, and playing brightly colored games where the only goal is to cut the most fruit or cause explosions with angry birds.

In many circles today, intelligence, introspection, and understanding are not only undervalued but also mocked as being nerdy, unimportant, or a waste of time compared to monetary gain, popularity, and status. Even when culture does attempt to promote self-discovery, education, or introspection, it comes in shallow forms like cheap self-help books and cursory personality tests.

I am a man with no degree and severe learning disabilities—but I still believe that if I am to be a fully good man, I must include learning and wisdom as two of my values.

But what is true wisdom and learning? Is it a master's degree? Is it a high IQ score? Is it knowing the biggest and most complicated words? Perhaps.

But I put forth that true wisdom isn't a piece of paper on a wall or a particular score on a test; it's taking ownership of your mind, informing your understanding, and beginning a never-ending journey to discovering truth—to better think, speak, act, and understand the world around us and the Creator who designed us.

We were created with the capacity to learn and understand. We were endowed with natural curiosity about the world around us, and to suppress that for the sake of comfort or distraction is to ignore the natural and fulfilling call to create and utilize our minds to their full potential. Even with my insecurities, I choose not to take the easy road of allowing a smartphone and others to think for me. Instead, I take ownership of the mind I have been given and do everything I can to cultivate it and use it to its full potential.

God has designed a beautiful universe filled with mystery and wonder that beckons us to experience its inherent majesty. But it's an offer we must choose to take: deciding to become curious about the world around us and using the mind and soul inside of us; learning to listen to men wiser than us; and chasing down questions, like hunting for treasure, that lead to beautiful answers.

In Proverbs, wisdom is portrayed as a woman calling to a man. She leads him on a chase and invites his pursuit. Her compelling voice places a passion within the man to follow and find her, and he ultimately wins her heart. Chasing a woman is a concept many of us guys can understand. And like pursuing a woman, pursuing wisdom takes time, thought, effort, and determination. And in the end, we find it is worth the effort as we are blessed by something good that makes life fuller and more beautiful.

This picture that Solomon paints is a beautiful image of how we ought to take the invitation to seek wisdom and ultimately make it our lifelong partner. The Proverbs are filled with words pointing to the importance of wisdom and the difference it makes in our lives. Solomon, the king of Israel, knew the danger of ignoring truth. When he was offered the chance to request anything from God, he asked for wisdom. And for this he was blessed.

Becoming wise isn't about being the smartest guy in the room. You know the kind—the one who rattles off inane factoids to impress or condescend. Wisdom is the conduit for living a healthy life. It has the power to make a meaningful difference in a lost and confused world, bringing joy to our days, understanding to our problems, and clarity to ourselves and the ones around us. When we take up the journey of learning, we'll see that our lives make more sense and we'll gain a larger and more complete perspective—one God Himself invites us to.

Although I never felt as smart as my parents or siblings, I was lucky enough to be in a family that measured intelligence not by a grade on a test or a score on a paper but by a desire in the heart. Early on, my mom and dad saw that I struggled to learn in the same way others naturally do. But instead of giving up and accepting the lie that wisdom wasn't something I needed, they found creative ways to complement how God had specifically designed me.

When my siblings would go read their books silently and I just couldn't sit still or quiet my mind, my mom would read books out loud to me while I drew pictures of the stories, enabling me to learn and grow my mind in my own unique way. Even today, while I still struggle to read for long periods at a time, I don't use that as an excuse to avoid learning. Instead, I'll pull out a drawing pad and listen to audiobooks, podcasts, and lectures that expand my mind in ways that work for me.

We need not compare ourselves or our learning styles with others. Instead, we must find the way we were made to learn and grow the mind God has given us.

I know of a secret place in Central Park. It's on top of a giant boulder with a large cutout in the hard, gray rock where I would sit back against the stone, hidden from the world and protected from the sun by the tree that grows around it. I won't tell you where it is; it's my secret place. But each weekday when I was living in the city, rain or shine, I would venture out of my studio apartment to my secret place.

I would plop down my black canvas backpack and pull out a granola bar, a bottle of iced tea, my sketch pad filled with drawings of the characters I saw around me each day, and a handful of books by authors old and new, each with unique perspectives on life, love, faith, humor, psychology, philosophy, humanity, and God. I would slowly work my way through the books' pages, opening my mind to the new and beautiful understanding I found within their words.

I was never good in classrooms. I was always too talkative, too fidgety, and too distracted to learn well in those spaces. It was the same with cubicles and small offices. But having been given a vision throughout my life of the importance of learning, I have fashioned my own classrooms where I can engage in learning and education the way I was designed to.

In addition to my Central Park hideaway, these classrooms have been secluded corners of cafés, the gray couch in my apartment (with me propped up on a million pillows), or even a desk shoved into a closet, where I could shut the door and get lost in podcasts and YouTube lectures.

When you gain wisdom and create a dedication to learning, you don't have to look like the man next to you, the scholar on TV, or even your family. It isn't about a particular place or piece of paper. Instead, it's about realizing the value of intelligence, deep thought, new perspectives, and truth. A wise man isn't always a good man, but a good man must be a wise man. Our dedication to learning and discovering truth is our responsibility. When we start the journey to better our minds and expand our intellectual vision, we will find ourselves able to walk the path to becoming good men with more light, vision, and perspective.

Questions for Reflection

1. Do you think intelligence, deep thought, and wisdom are important and necessary parts of becoming a good man?

2. What things in your life keep you from pursuing learning?

3. What are a few ways you can begin to own your education? What are your favorite ways to learn? Podcasts? Videos? Books?

> My father taught me,
> "Take my words to heart.
>> Follow my commands, and you will live.
> Get wisdom; develop good judgment.
>> Don't forget my words or turn away from them.
> Don't turn your back on wisdom, for she will protect
>> you.
>> Love her, and she will guard you.
> Getting wisdom is the wisest thing you can do!
>> And whatever else you do, develop good judgment.
> If you prize wisdom, she will make you great.
>> Embrace her, and she will honor you.
> She will place a lovely wreath on your head;
>> she will present you with a beautiful crown."
>
> Proverbs 4:4–9

THE WISE MAN

God of all knowledge and truth, help us with our limited
faculties to see Your wisdom more clearly each day.

Entrenched in each of us is the desire
to know, to learn, and to find.
This is not so we can bolster ourselves or our egos,
but so we can better move and act in ways that
bring clarity through our lives, healing through our
words, and perspective through our actions.

Let us cast off the temptation to settle for the indifferent
and thoughtless existence the world offers so freely.
And let us instead take up the torch of knowledge
that will shed Your light of truth in dark places.
Let us not be taken by the world's convoluted and
haughty laws, but instead let us see Your face and
hear Your voice more clearly, that we may better
understand and know You as our Creator.

Thank You for our minds and that You have endowed
us with an endless capacity to grow in wisdom. May
we be good stewards of what You have graciously
given us while humbly knowing Your thoughts are above
our thoughts and Your ways are above our ways.

Amen.

ELEVEN

Ambitious

Our ambition should be to rule ourselves, the true kingdom for each one of us; and true progress is to know more, and be more, and to do more.

Oscar Wilde

I am fully aware that the statement I am about to make will put me squarely in nerd territory, but here it goes: I love video games. I love them mostly because I love stories, and video games allow me to totally immerse myself in a story—one I could normally live out only in my dreams. I mean, people might give me funny looks if I wore a hood and carried around a sword in search of ancient treasure. But in a game, I can live out an epic tale in a way I simply can't in my modern life.

I especially love a game called Skyrim, an open-world adventure where upon choosing your character you are thrust into a realm of dragons, sword fights, and nonstop exploring. You and the choices you make affect the entire narrative. With every new quest, you uncover a bit more of the grand tale being told. It may involve exploring a forgotten kingdom, fighting a dragon, saving a fair lady, or even becoming a king. But every turn and twist leads you onward and upward through an unraveling narrative.

I see the irony in exposing my love for video games in a chapter titled "Ambitious." All too often young men are known to waste hours, and even years, with their eyes glued to a screen in a dark basement, surrounded by junk food wrappers and far from the blinding light of day.

And this is where I found myself after graduating from high school.

All my friends had left for college, and since my future hadn't yet made itself clear, I found myself in a sudden wave of depression. I longed for a meaningful and adventurous life, like the ones the characters in the video games lived. But facing an uncertain path, I retreated into my basement, where I spent countless hours in front of a screen, stuffing candy bars and chips into my mouth. I disappeared into adventures that fulfilled, at least in small part, my intrinsic desire to do something great.

In my heart I wanted more. I wanted to be part of something great. I wanted to use my passions and skills for something bigger than my small-town, inexperienced mind could imagine. But I felt lost. I didn't know how to bridge the gap between where I was and where I wanted to be.

After several months, I was forty pounds overweight, depressed, and lost. The only thing that hadn't changed was the burning desire in my soul for something more. So late one night, fed up with where I was and who I was becoming, I shut off the TV, got up off the couch (that now had an indent of my body in it), stepped over the empty bottles and junk food wrappers, and pulled up the browser on my computer. This was my first step in living out the story I wanted to tell with my life in the real world.

I knew I loved stories, movies, books, and games. I had a strong imagination and a gift for performing, so I got on the internet and started looking for places and ways I could use my passions and skills.

Six months later I found myself in NYC at my first "acting for film" class at a film school. I took my first steps onto the path I had created, and now, ten years later, I haven't looked back.

My decision that night to get up off the couch has led me around the world to countless movie and TV sets and numerous stages and connected me with unique, inspiring people. It's opened doors and helped me find something that uses the gifts I was born with. By simply making the choice to *do something*, I began a lifelong journey I could've once only imagined in my dreams.

As I look back, I can see that my love for games, movies, and books was rooted in who I was made to be. God created me with talents and passions I was always meant to live out. But I had to take that first step of getting up and doing something.

If we truly believe we were designed by a thoughtful and meticulous Creator, it only makes sense that we were designed for a purpose. Every great invention or beautiful work of art was meant to do, invoke, or become something. They have purpose and meaning in this world. They were put together for a reason. So are we. We each have been made with unique gifts, skills, and personalities for a reason. God, the great Creator, has given each of us a calling in this world—a calling that is greater than ourselves and draws us to the story He has for us to tell.

While on earth, Jesus constantly talked about the kingdom of God. This confused many of His followers, as He was a wanderer who walked the streets and had no money to His name. What kind of kingdom was that? But as we pore through the words and life of Jesus, we find a more beautiful kingdom than the one we've come to know in this world. The kingdom Jesus was talking about isn't about strong armies, land mass, and wealth; instead, it revolves around love, beauty, forgiveness, joy, and peace. It requires no gold and instead asks for our entire lives.

God has created each of us with a place in this kingdom. Just like the roles I play in the video games, each one of us has been asked to play our character in the story He is weaving. It's a story in which our choices make an eternal difference and we have a small part in something bigger than we could possibly imagine.

When I heard the "Kingdom of God" talk as a kid, I was sure that the kingdom roles were all filled by pastors and missionaries. But if we look in the Bible, we find God's kingdom encompasses so much more. It's something that resides in the hearts of all of us, and we are called to use our gifts and passions for the new, redeemed world God is creating.

I found freedom when I realized that my love of stories, acting, and art isn't just a random interest for my own selfish gain but a calling uniquely placed on my heart to be used for a story greater than one I could tell on my own. I began to see how my talents and passions could be used to love, redeem, and bring hope to a dark, desperate world. The things I loved were the very things God had placed there so I could take part in His story.

But because God is a gentleman, I was never forced, only asked, to use my life and gifts for Him. It was my decision to make. And it took me actually getting up off my couch to pursue the things I loved and then connecting with my Creator as I learned how to use each of my gifts for the kingdom.

In Matthew 25:14–30, Jesus told a parable about a master and three servants. The master decided to give his servants *talents* (the Hebrew word for *coin*, which ironically works perfectly for this parable). One man was given five talents, one man two talents, and another man one talent. The man with five talents invested his talents and ended up doubling the gift he had been given. The second man with two talents did the same, but the third man buried his talent in the ground. When their master returned, the first two men showed what they had done with what they were given, and the master praised them and blessed them with more. But when the third man handed back the talent he had been given, it was covered in dirt, never having been invested or used. The master was disappointed and angry and sent the man away.

Having the gifts, skills, and personality we have isn't random, and it isn't just for our own good. We have a calling and responsibility to use what we have for a purpose bigger than ourselves.

We weren't made to sit around and wait until we die. We were made to *do something*.

––––––––

Nihilism is the belief that, ultimately, there is no God, moral responsibility, or meaning to life. We are here randomly, and since we all will die and our consciousness will fade into oblivion, there is no point in doing, well . . . anything. This worldview has seeped into our culture in a potent and destructive way, affecting the men of this generation like a cancer. It whispers to us to ignore hard work and meaningful lives and to chase only lives of comfort and pleasure, to do whatever feels good, to do whatever we can get away with—because why not? We're all going to die.

But in reality, as we step away from this bitter and lazy worldview, we see that it is simply a drug that feeds into the darker side of our humanity, a drug that lulls us into believing that everything is meaningless and there's no point to getting up off the couch and chasing a better and more meaningful life.

From The Lord of the Rings to Star Wars, from The Matrix to Superman, every popular hero story involves a choice. It's a choice that calls the heroes to a great story in which their natural gifts serve a greater purpose. And while we have no magic rings, lightsabers, or superpowers, we each have embedded within us something meaningful to offer the world.

Our choice is whether we ignore our calling and idly wait for death as so many men do today or accept a role as one of the "chosen ones," living out our destiny as a character in a story bigger than ourselves.

This won't look the same in all of our lives, and that's a beautiful thing. The story you were made to tell isn't the one I was made to tell. But you have a story to live, and it starts with a choice to do something. I don't know what that choice is for you—maybe it's filling out the job or school application that's been sitting on your desk, maybe it's writing the novel you've been daydreaming about since high school, maybe it's gathering up the courage to finally ask out the cute girl you see every day at the café, or maybe it's deciding to dream about what it is you want to do.

Taking that first step is not easy. Like any good thing, it will take time, bravery, risk, learning from failures, practice, getting up when you fall, and years of dedication. But every drop of sweat, every cramped muscle, every hard lesson learned will ultimately push you further into the story you were made to tell. Every truly great hero, whether fictional or historical, made a choice to do something. You can too.

Questions for Reflection

1. What are the things you naturally enjoy and find interesting? Could any of the things you listed become life-long, meaningful passions?
2. How could they be used in a way that helps the world and honors God?
3. What keeps you from doing them? What can you do to jump these hurdles?

> Lazy people want much but get little,
> but those who work hard will prosper.
>
> Proverbs 13:4

THE MAN OF ACTION

God, who in Your greatness was the first to
act and bring about all life, let us look to You
and Your example as we seek to follow in Your
footsteps and bring life into our world.
Give us a vision for how we may use our lives, our time,
and our ability to expand Your ever-growing kingdom.

Thank You that You are a God who moves and acts
with consistency and regularity in the lives of the
ones You love and the world You have created.
Help us learn the art of taking responsibility for the
gifts You have given us, using them in ways that will
bring about more goodness to Your creation.

Let us not run away from the dreams, passions, and skills
You have given us. Show us how we might use them more
fully in the beautiful work You have given us to do.

Thank You that You allow us to be part of the story
You are telling and for the spiritual, mental, and
physical gifts You have graciously given each of
us to use for a purpose bigger than ourselves.

Help us overcome lethargy, anxiety, fear, and pride
as we choose to actively engage with the world and
souls around us to better bring about Your kingdom.

Amen.

Fighting

When I say it's you I like, I'm talking about that part of you that knows that life is far more than anything you can ever see or hear or touch. That deep part of you that allows you to stand for those things without which humankind cannot survive. Love that conquers hate, peace that rises triumphant over war, and justice that proves more powerful than greed.

Fred Rogers

I've only been punched in the face a handful of times (pun intended), and usually these hits were well deserved.

When I was a teen in my little Colorado town, one of my troublemaking friends tossed a firework into a crowd of people at a big festival, causing surprise and rousing the ire of two drunk guys. My friend ran, but I stood my ground and said something snarky. Seconds later I woke up in the gravel with a throbbing jaw and a cut on my cheek that I later blamed on my dog. There's some fight in most guys. Even in nature we watch as bucks slam their antlers into each other, wolves wrestle, and monkeys beat their chests. This fighting instinct is natural, but it can be misused and cause great and needless damage.

I wanted to be a good kid, but I had all this pent-up testosterone and youthful idiocy that kept me finding myself in less-than-ideal situations. Watching action stars struggle and fight in movies struck a chord with me. I wanted to fight, win, and conquer—and it kept getting me into trouble.

At one point, after watching a movie and being quite taken with it, my friends and I had the great idea to start a fight club. We held it in my family's basement, where in friendly competition we beat the snot out of each other until someone conceded or broke something—like my friend Matt, who smashed fists with Jeff, breaking his hand. We would emerge bruised and beaten, but we felt like warriors. To this day there are still blood-stains on the carpet in our home.

I'm older now and get into less fights—only the occasional war of words with a telemarketer or a keyboard vigilante who must be proven wrong—but I still feel that "something" deep down that makes me want to be a fighter. I still feel the rush of adrenaline when I get cast in a role that allows me to yell, run, and choreograph fight scenes. It wasn't long ago that I acted in a fight scene for a movie that required me to punch the bad guy repeatedly. As I threw my fists at the other actor while the camera rolled, I was surprised by how naturally it came. The thing is, I don't think I'm the only one with this kind of fight in me.

Regardless of their stature, many of the best men I've known feel the same intrinsic pull to fight. It's why we see countless superhero and action movies, each with bigger battles, being eaten up by eager audiences and making billions of dollars each year. It's why boxing matches make millions of dollars as people shell out cash for a pay-per-view pass to see two fighters clash for an hour. It's why we see swaths of young men addicted to video games through which they can take up their swords/laser guns/lightsabers and become champions in imaginary worlds.

Even online we witness a never-ending array of what we might call trolls, people fighting not with fists but with words. I wonder if they're trying to satisfy their natural instinct to fight something, anything. We're often told this is bad, that we should suppress the fight within us. And this is understandably so, especially when we see it manifest in dark and destructive ways. But it seems we are left in a catch-22. We have a natural desire for "the fight," but it often turns ugly and destructive.

As good men, what are we to do?

I guess we could suppress this desire, as many would argue. Or we could give in to it and continue fighting meaningless battles that bring about nothing but destruction. I humbly offer that we were designed to travel another road.

Toward the end of Jesus's life on earth, the bad guys came to take Him away. One of His closest friends, Peter, pulled out a sword and chopped off one of the bad guys' ears. Instead of encouraging more violence, Jesus stopped His followers from fighting and told them as He healed the bleeding bad guy, "Those who use the sword will die by the sword" (Matt. 26:52). Earlier, when faced with an enemy, Jesus told His disciples to love their enemies instead of hurting them. If the disciples were slapped in the face, Jesus said for them to "turn to them the other cheek also" (Matt. 5:39 NIV). These stories frustrated his disciples and they frustrate me. Each of those men had fight inside them, fight that God Himself had put there, and here was Jesus telling them not to use it!

But another story about Jesus also gets brought up when talking about His peaceful ways. It throws a wrench in our understanding of who God is and how He works. Jesus walked into the temple with a whip and flipped the tables and drove out a bunch of crooks. I love this story because it's not black-and-white no matter how much we want it to be—there's nuance and tension. All through His life, Jesus confused and baffled those around Him, as He still does today.

But Jesus wasn't confused at all Himself. His actions were not contradictory; they were exactly in line with who He is and who He asks us to be. Just like Jesus, this issue of our natural inclination versus our call to be peacemakers is not entirely obvious at first glance. But if we look a little closer, we just might find the way we are meant to live this tension out in the world.

When looking at the story of Jesus, so often I feel we project on Him what we want to justify about our own lives. The violent will say He was a man of war, and the pacifists will say He was a gentle hippie. But what if He wasn't either? What if He, like us, had fight in Him, but He knew how, why, and where to use it?

Jesus was both a man of peace and someone who stood up to violent authority. He was a fighter and also allowed Himself to be crucified. And it seems to me that when He stood up and fought, it was rarely for Himself, always for a good reason, and meant to accomplish something better that just bragging rights.

Meaning, perhaps our drive to fight is for a greater purpose than just fighting for the sake of fighting. Perhaps we were given this desire and ability to fight for peace and protection. I think to live as good men, we don't want to deny or suppress something God has so obviously put inside of us, but instead we should learn how best to use it.

I firmly believe we have the choice to use our strength to be either predators or protectors. We have the ability to either utilize our fight to bring order and guard beauty in the world or to cause more chaos and brokenness. We get to decide how to use this gift God has given us. In our culture today, which is soaked with pride and bravado, it can be difficult to use this gift in positive and healthy ways.

But throughout history, the men who have bridled their aggression and sought ways to use their natural proclivity to fight for good (either physically, mentally, or verbally) have changed the world for the better.

Think of Martin Luther King Jr., who fought for a higher good through nonviolent activism and championed for the civil rights of black Americans. Or Army Corporal Desmond Doss, who refused to kill an enemy soldier or carry a weapon into combat and saved seventy-five men in one of the bloodiest battles of WWII. These men showed us that true heroism and fighting doesn't have to include violence. And even when this broken world forces us into a physical altercation, we participate only as a last resort and for a greater purpose—to protect innocence and preserve God's beauty.

I still remember so clearly seeing the difference between the good guys and the bad guys the first time I sat down with my dad to watch the first Star Wars movie. The Dark Side (the bad guys), in their black cloaks and red lightsabers, would tell their recruits to carry anger and hatred. But the Light Side (the good guys) encouraged peace, temperance, and order while letting go of anger and revenge.

When we accept the gift we have been given as men to fight for something, then lay it down as an offering to our Creator, we begin to see why we were created with this inclination and how God wants us to use it. As we become good men, God shows us how to fight and, more important, why. Learning to fight the right way, the way we were designed to, protects and brings value to the world instead of chaos and destruction. It requires self-control, temperance, wisdom, intellect, character, and a desire for peace and harmony.

In reality, we wage day-to-day wars not on the battlefield but in our own everyday lives. Each of us will face battles this week and this month.

We can choose to fight for good when we stand up for a kid at school who is being bullied.

We can choose to fight for good when we forgive someone who hurt us, even if they don't deserve it.

We can choose to fight for good when we get involved with fighting sex trafficking instead of watching porn.

We can choose to fight for good when we refuse to give in to hopelessness and reach out for help to manage our anxieties and obsessive thoughts.

We can choose to fight for good by showing a vulnerable woman protection, care, and the love of Jesus.

Or maybe our fight for good is simply not picking up another drink, cigarette, or fast-food meal as we seek to become better men.

Whatever the fight you're facing right now—big or small, long-lasting or momentary, difficult or easy—know this: God has put fight in you for a reason, and good men are called to hone their skills and use that fight for good.

Let's learn to be warriors who fight for something better. Let's learn to stand up when we need to let go of pride, anger, and hate and keep our eye on the real prize of protecting good and bringing peace. It's then that we will be fighting in the very way God fights for us.

Questions for Reflection

1. What battle are you fighting right now?
2. How can you learn to fight the way God created you to, not the way the world tells you to?
3. Do you ever feel like you suppress your inclination to fight, even in healthy ways? Why?

> Better to be patient than powerful;
> better to have self-control than to conquer a city.
>
> Proverbs 16:32

THE FIGHTER

God, who is eternally strong and powerful
but also tender and kind, help us follow Your
example as we enter the battles in this world.

Give us the courage to fight when necessary, a
vision to know what to fight for, and the wisdom
to know how to fight in a way that brings about
Your everlasting kingdom of peace and does not
add to the world's crumbling kingdom of chaos.

Teach us daily to make the choice to turn
the other cheek while standing up for the
innocent in the likeness of Jesus's example.

Let us cast off pride, ego, and selfishness and
take up humility, forgiveness, and gentleness—
even in the midst of our battles.

Let us remember that our battle is against not flesh
and blood but enemies of spiritual darkness that will
be defeated only by Your light, love, and truth.

Thank You that when Jesus could've won the fight
against His captors, He instead chose to win the war
by laying down His life so that we could be free.

Amen.

THIRTEEN

Simple

And the world cannot be discovered by a journey of miles, no matter how long, but only by a spiritual journey, a journey of one inch, very arduous and humbling and joyful, by which we arrive at the ground at our own feet, and learn to be at home.

Wendell Berry

I'm currently sitting on my couch, covered in a sleeping bag, playing video games, and watching Netflix in between forced bursts of energy to type away on an old hand-me-down laptop. There are empty frozen meal and ramen containers on the table, next to a mug that has been filled with coffee, not two but three times today. The laundry needs to be folded, and my taxes are sitting ignored on the kitchen table in my shared studio apartment, which I haven't left once today.

Everything feels normal, too normal. This isn't the adventurous and meaningful life I thought I had signed up for when I decided to follow God into becoming the man I was made to be. The whole scene is only made more ironic by my wearing a Superman shirt my mom gave me last Christmas. I feel anything but super in this small moment.

As I've mentioned, I've loved Superman since I was kid. I longed to live a life like his, making a difference in the world and doing something that truly mattered. I knew that (most likely) I wouldn't be able to fly, run faster than a speeding bullet, or bend steel. But still, somewhere in my heart, I longed for the great story. This desire is built into the hearts of all men.

So why am I here working on the couch I also sleep on instead of fighting foes? What's going on? Where's my epic story? Am I not good enough for an exciting life? Am I just not made for greatness like others are? Like the ones I see on TV, read about in books and magazines, and envy on social media?

In the midst of my crisis of normalcy, I am suddenly struck by part of the Superman story that isn't always told. Typically, the name Superman ignites scenes of action and adventure in our minds, but what about the man behind Superman, Clark Kent? What is Clark Kent's actual identity?

Clark Kent was normal. He grew up the son of a working man in the flat fields of a flyover state and spent most of his early years going to school and doing farm chores (albeit superly), and eventually he landed a job as a newspaper reporter.

One of the things I think I love so much about the Superman story isn't Superman at all; it's the simple man behind the glasses. I love that Clark Kent is just a regular guy. It helps me believe that maybe there is still hope for something great to be found amid my seemingly uneventful days and in the future. It gives me hope that perhaps there is value in not only catching bullets but the everyday things.

When Jesus, at the age of thirty, went into the world to do His "work," He called men to help Him. But while gathering His "league" to save the world, He didn't go looking for superheroes. He didn't seek the important politicians or powerful soldiers. Instead, He chose the normal men of His age to join Him in the world-changing work.

Jesus invited fishermen, tax collectors, and shepherds. They constantly bugged Him about raising up a revolution, starting an army, and living out the visions in their minds. But Jesus had a very different vision for changing the world, and it started with simple community, talking to loved ones, eating food on the beach, befriending the outcasts, and feeding the homeless. Jesus, God Himself, spent the majority of His adult life as a simple salt-of-the-earth, dirt-beneath-His-fingernails carpenter.

I wonder if Jesus ever looked up from His tools, wiped the sweat from His brow with His splinter-filled hands, and anxiously wished for His exciting life to begin. Or did He know that He was right where He was supposed to be. I wonder if He ever longed for more exciting times or if He was perfectly content knowing that in normalcy lay the world-changing mission He had come to earth to fulfill.

When the God of everything was born, He was overlooked by many who were waiting for the great leader to come riding in on a horse in a suit of armor and with a sword in His hand. Instead, He came as a baby, born to a teenage mother, and spent many years as a simple carpenter.

Life can be so, for lack of a better word, boring. I know all too well the deep longing and anxious desire for something *more*, for adventure to crash through my tedious day-to-day work and give me the epic life I've always wanted. I know all too well the insecurity when looking at the mundane trappings of my life and having the sneaky thought that I'm just not cut out for a grand story.

I see other guys reaching the heights of what our world now calls *greatness*. I hear stories of billionaires by thirty, breakout teenage actors, and influencers living in exotic places I dream of visiting. And while the desire for greatness is God-given and good, when we look at the people of the Bible, history, and fiction, what we so often see is an abundance of normal. God seems to like using normal people to accomplish His world-changing missions, often through very normal means. And it makes me think that God's view of greatness is a lot simpler than ours.

———

We live in a world that celebrates the highlight reel. But as a writer and actor, I spend much of my time in the in-between. For every movie role and premiere, there are months of waiting for the phone to ring. For every book release, there are sometimes years of writing alone, looking for inspiration in the quiet moments. In fact, most of our lives are lived in the in-between, and it's no less meaningful or important. It's where we find out who we really are and what it means to be human; it's where we create the memories worth recording and capture the thoughts worth writing about.

If you are in an in-between, remember that life isn't lived only in the highlights. Embracing the season of waiting can be meaningful, and it can be the place you find who you truly are.

An in-between moment may be experiencing connection and meaning while laughing with friends over an inside joke, eating a home-cooked meal with your family, enjoying a movie with your significant other, or relishing a quiet moment alone with your Creator. These are what a true and beautiful life is made of. And in the end, the highlights are just lovely detours in the life you were made to live.

We all long for a great and meaningful life, but the more I look at the "heroes," whether they are from the Bible, history, or fiction, the more I see that their lives began not with a loud whirlwind of exciting happenings but a million little whispers of day-to-day life.

It's easy to fall into the trap of thinking we're not measuring up to the world's standards of greatness. I've wanted to be a hero in an epic story all of my life, but what if my concept of a hero and an epic story isn't the same as God's? If you look at Jesus's life, you'll see that He's one of the most influential people in history. But a majority of His life was very normal.

Perhaps our own journey begins not out there in some grand adventure but in our everyday monotony—our jobs, our small-town churches, our imperfect families, and our messy houses. Perhaps our epic quest starts not with saving the damsel in distress but with loving our wives. Maybe it begins not with meeting kings but with respecting our bosses, not with preaching to millions but reaching out to a friend in need, not with slaying dragons but feeding the homeless man on our street.

God has called each of us to a great life, but we don't have to wait to begin that life. We start our great life right now, in the normalcy of day-to-day living. We can live great lives by loving our neighbor, serving our family, and remaining constant, trustworthy people.

God loves using the normal for His epic story. Normal circumstances, normal men. This is good news, because your great life is waiting to begin right here, right now, right where you are.

Questions for Reflection

1. What misconceptions do you have about "greatness"?
2. How can you begin to look at your life as meaningful, right now?
3. Do you believe God uses normal people in normal circumstances for greatness?

> Make it your goal to live a quiet life, minding your own business and working with your hands, just as we instructed you before.
>
> 1 Thessalonians 4:11

A PRAYER FOR
THE SIMPLE

God, thank You that while being God incarnate,
Creator of the universe and maker of the heavens,
You came to us through Your Son, Jesus, and lived a
simple and unencumbered life. In Your Scripture, we
find an example of how to live by how Jesus lived on
earth—not worrying about monetary gain, chasing
power, or becoming entangled in the other trappings
of the world but instead eating with friends, loving the
people around Him, and working with His hands.

Thank You that even in the simplicity of life You
are near and Your epic story is unfolding in the
mundane, day-to-day work You have given us.

While You have called us to dream big dreams
and live lives of greatness, let us never forget
that we can begin right here in our homes, meals,
conversations, quiet times, and daily lives.

Thank You for using the humble and poor in spirit
to accomplish Your work on earth. Help us learn
to live and love the way Jesus did and see You
in the small, normal, everyday moments.

Amen.

FOURTEEN

Servant-Hearted

The measure of a man's greatness is not the number of
servants he has, but the number of people he serves.

John Hagee

I was troubled when I was seventeen. I was a headstrong and
proud young man. I had a desire in my heart to be good, to
follow God and live a great story, but it was buried somewhere
inside of me, overshadowed by my adolescent antics. I ran in a
little group of guys with too much testosterone and free time
and not developed enough brains to make wise decisions.

Interestingly enough, I met these guys at church. I sat next
to Matt, Ben, and Chad at youth group one night, and Matt
leaned over and asked if I wanted a Starburst. I did. The rest
was history. We had good hearts, but with youth comes pride.
On Wednesday nights and Sunday mornings we would be raising our hands and jumping to the latest worship song, then

on Friday nights we'd be racing cars while blaring rock music, kissing girls, swearing, and smoking cherry cigars.

We had a desire in our hearts to be good men and set ourselves apart from the world in a positive way, but the pull of youthful stupidity was strong, and in a tug-of-war between responsibility and youthful arrogance, the latter often won. However, even with our noisy teenage attitudes, we all decided to join a church small group, maybe as a dare to ourselves or maybe as an unconscious response to that voice in our hearts. We ended up in an accountability group that met on Sunday nights at the house of a college student named Stefan.

About ten of us would sit around and talk about God and the sins we were struggling with. Though when my turn came, I offered more boasts and brags than confessions. Still, Stefan kept inviting us back, opening his home to a bunch of rowdy high school boys because he wanted us to know God and become better men, even if it meant putting up with our shenanigans.

It's hard to imagine the frustration he may have felt at taking the time and effort to try to reach a bunch of cocky teenage boys with uninformed opinions about the world, but still he did it. Maybe he had a feeling it was worthwhile, that it would ultimately make a difference even if he couldn't see it yet.

We attended the small group for a couple of years, and often I wonder if it looked as though we were making no progress at all. But there, in the actions of serving us, listening to our teenage anxiety, and being a present and willing example of a good man, Stefan was making a difference in our lives despite the arrogance I proudly wore on my cutoff sleeves.

I spent many memorable times in that small group. Times of catharsis, laughter, and even occasional learning. But out of those two years, one night in particular stands out.

It began like most of our evenings together—loud laughter, talk about girls, and overall goofing around. But as the meeting began, Stefan pulled out a large bowl of water and some clean, dry cloths. We looked at one another, intrigued. He asked us to sit down in some chairs he had set up in the middle of the room and take off our shoes. Then he proceeded to work his way down the line, washing each of our feet. Our leader, the one who had years of wisdom and spiritual authority on us, knelt down and washed and dried our stinky teenage toes.

To some this might sound like some sort of weird ritual, and I get it. It comes from the beautiful story found in the Bible where Jesus, on the eve of His death, washed His disciples' feet. In those days, it was something only a lowly servant would do—going near the dirty and sweat-stained feet of working men. But before Jesus died for His friends, He served them. He knelt as an example of what real love is and what good men ought to do.

The story is detailed in John 13:3–5:

> Jesus knew that the Father had given him authority over everything and that he had come from God and would return to God. So he got up from the table, took off his robe, wrapped a towel around his waist, and poured water into a basin. Then he began to wash the disciples' feet, drying them with the towel he had around him.

As I look back on that night when Stefan knelt and washed our feet, it's a picture to me of what a true and good man does.

It's a picture of what the best man, Jesus, did for His disciples and is willing to do for all of us.

———————

Living in both LA and NYC, I've had to face the cultural values of both cities. There's a lot of pride, ego, and material status. I've been confronted by people showing off who they are and what they have. I drive an old, beat-up Honda I've had since I was sixteen, and I remember driving it down the streets of Hollywood next to the brand-new, shiny sports cars. I've felt out of place and underdressed in my white T-shirt and Goodwill jacket, walking next to teenagers covered in name-brand clothes. I've experienced the sting of disappointment when comparing my humble career to those who are younger, richer, and more successful than I am. I've been on sets with "stars" who refuse to talk to or look at extras. And I've heard the phrase "Do you know who I am?" more than I'd like to admit.

I'm not immune. I catch myself trying to show and tell people how great I am, highlighting my best moments, hiding my worst, bragging and exaggerating about things to feel more important and make others feel less than me. I don't like it about myself, and I don't like it about these towns, but deep within every one of us is a seed of pride that wants to believe we're better than others. When we feel the sneaking insecurity that we're not, we so often overcompensate, hoping to soothe our fragile egos.

But at the end of the day, when I finally sit down in my dimly lit studio, away from the noise of the streets and the shining lights of the city, and open the book about the Jewish carpenter I (try) to follow, I'm confronted with a staggeringly different life philosophy. It stands in stark contrast to the image of the modern man I am surrounded by, the one I am so often tempted to become.

In Jesus I find a picture of the Creator of the universe, the maker of the stars and time, stepping down into our broken world, being born in a manger, living a life of loving and serving others, making food for the hungry, touching the sick, healing the broken, and ultimately dying for people who turned their backs on Him. It's a picture of things He has done, and things He continues to do, for me even when I turn my back on Him.

The one man who had every right to brag about who He was, show off what He could do, and demand service from others humbled Himself to love and give everything He had to those (us—you, me) who could do nothing to deserve it.

So how do we reconcile culture's version of a modern man with a humble and meek carpenter who chose to put others ahead of Himself? Do we dog ourselves and self-flagellate to remind us of how bad we are? I don't think so. I don't think that works. I've tried the false humility, but it's just that—false. I found that when I practiced it too much, I quickly drifted into self-loathing, which isn't something Jesus wants, practiced, or ever asked for. It might be a shortcut to *looking* humble, but being truly humble isn't thinking bad things about yourself; it's thinking beautiful things about others.

Jesus knew He was God, but He didn't pretend He was less than He was or use a false humility to downgrade Himself. Instead, fully knowing who He was, what He had, and what He could do, He thought deeply of others and how to love them more. It's easy to say things, but it's hard to do them. Looking humble is one thing, but being humble and actually putting it into practice takes effort.

But for those of us on a journey to becoming good men, it's a worthwhile effort.

I remember how hard my parents worked from the time I was very young. In addition to writing fifteen books and speaking around the world, my mom worked tirelessly to love and care for our family. She cooked meals, cleaned messes, caught tears, and home educated all of us. In addition to being a pastor, my dad worked long hours at the office to keep the family ministry going and ensure we were provided for.

At the end of each day, I recall how my dad would notice how tired my mom was, so after dinner he would gather all the dishes and clean the kitchen. It was a small gesture, but it was meaningful. It gave her time to rest. He was thinking of her needs above his own. And he did this over and over and over again, giving young me a picture of what being a servant really is. He loved and followed the way and example of Jesus by modeling humility and servanthood.

In every example of servanthood I can think of, whether it involves my small-group leader, my dad, or Jesus, one person chose intentionally to see the needs, wants, and desires of someone else; one person decided to look past their own comfort and desires to give of their time, their effort, and themselves. Jesus provided the ultimate example of this when He gave everything for us. And He asks us to do the same for the people around us.

Whether it's washing dishes or washing feet, we each must think outside ourselves and focus on serving others if we are to combat our natural inclination toward pride and take hold of the life-changing value of servanthood. Being a strong man, an effective man, a good man requires humility—and humility requires action.

Most of us have trouble doing this. We are too caught up in the whirlwind of our own lives. But to be good men, we must humble ourselves and see others and their needs, even when it requires us to make a sacrifice. We don't do this because it's fun or easy, or because we fear judgment if we don't or expect praise if we do. We do this because the maker of heaven and earth, the maker of men Himself, does it for us.

In Matthew 20:26–28, Jesus tells us this:

> Not so with you. Instead, whoever wants to become great among you must be your servant, and whoever wants to be first must be your slave—just as the Son of Man did not come to be served, but to serve, and to give his life as a ransom for many. (NIV)

If our God and Creator does this for us, to be truly good men, we are called to do the same. We need not pretend we are worse than we are or conjure a false humility that helps no one. We need only to lay down our own pride so as to love others in the same way our God has loved us.

This will look different for each of us. For some it might look like serving our family after a long day or listening to a friend over a coffee or volunteering on our day off. But whatever way we choose to serve and humble ourselves before others, we do it because our God does it for us.

Questions for Reflection

1. Are humility and service important? Why or why not?
2. What are ways you can start thinking less of yourself and more of others?
3. What are your own obstacles to humility and serving others?

> For you have been called to live in freedom, my brothers and sisters. But don't use your freedom to satisfy your sinful nature. Instead, use your freedom to serve one another in love.
>
> Galatians 5:13

THE SERVANT-HEARTED

God, who shows us how to love, give, and
serve by loving, giving, and serving,
teach us to follow Jesus's example in thinking
beyond ourselves and serving the hurting and
needing world around us each day.

Give us a desire to love the fractured places in
the world and the hearts You have put in our
proximity. Break our hearts for what breaks
Yours, and give us eyes to see where we can act
as Your healing hands and feet to others.

You tell us that honor is reserved for the servant
of all; help us live humbly enough to desire higher
praise than the world offers by giving of ourselves,
our time, and our resources to those in need.

Give us eyes to see like You and a
heart to serve like You serve us.

Amen.

FIFTEEN

Committed

Our greatest glory is not in never falling, but in rising every time we fall.

Confucius

Dozens of miles outside the small mountain town of Breckenridge, Colorado, and hours away from any other kind of substantial civilization, there's a cutout in the road. You'll miss it if you're not looking for it, like I almost did that first time I pulled my car over. Only vehicles that have made a wrong turn or trucks hauling cargo pass by every now and again, taking little notice of a small dirt patch at the edge of the forest that leads into the middle of nowhere. But if you should find this cutout in the road, pull over, turn off the radio and your humming car engine, and take a breath. Step out of your car and feel the chill from the mountains sweep against your face. If you stand very still, you'll be confronted with the deafening silence of the Colorado wilderness.

I remember the first time I stood in that place, the wind moving down off the mountain, beckoning me toward a path at its base. Something inside me whispered that I needed to follow that path and, more important, find what lay at the end of it. The trail leads almost immediately into thick woods, and when I ventured in for the first time, having no schedule to abide by or pressing issues to address, I took my time, breathing in the surroundings. Whispering pines greeted me and ushered me farther up and farther in. I noticed patches of snow still lingering in the shade of the branches as I climbed the trail, steadily venturing up to an unknown destination.

It's hard to breathe at ten thousand feet, and often even the fittest people will find themselves stopping to catch their breath in the thin air of the Rockies. I have had asthma since I was a kid. I can remember waking up in the middle of the night gasping for air as my parents pulled out the machine that pumped oxygen into my tired lungs. But here there was no oxygen machine, only my curiosity and a will to explore that was stronger than my desire for the comfort of my car.

I could feel my breath getting shorter the farther I went. I slowed down but kept moving into the dark forest, along the uneven and rocky path that seemed to shift and break with every step I took. For half an hour I kept making my way slowly through the trees and up the mountain. Taking a breath, I stopped and lifted my eyes to the path ahead, where I saw a break in the trees. After a sip out of a water bottle and one more deep breath, I pressed on. Almost like there was an unseen landscaper clearing the forest, the trees simply stopped, and as I navigated past them, I realized I was moving beyond the timberline, to a place where no trees could grow.

I was breathing heavily, but I had made it out of the forest. I stopped to take in the next part of my journey. In front of me was a steep inclined field that stretched for a thousand feet, sharply leading up a hill covered in waving yellow grass and jutting rocks. I stood looking at the climb in front of me, wondering if perhaps I had adventured enough for one day. My lungs were already tired. But again, I heard a still, small voice telling me to keep going, to not give up, that the end would be worth it. So I did.

I took one more deep breath, gathering as much oxygen as my lungs could take from the thin air, and pressed onward and upward. The steep grade made it hard to find footing. More than once or twice my foothold gave way and I fell to the ground, landing on my hands and knees. The sharp rocks stung my palms and bits of blood could be seen in the scrapes. After the third fall, my knees were skinned beneath my torn jeans and I thought perhaps I should just give up, climb down the incline, and call it a day.

But again, that inner voice whispered, "Keep going."

I caught my breath, pushed myself back up, and pressed on. The farther I climbed, the harder it was to breathe but the easier it was to convince myself to keep going. After an hour of fighting the mountain, the dry brown grass jutting from the rocky dirt receded behind me and I found my footing on bigger and bigger rocks. The incline was beginning to level out, and just a few hundred feet in front of me, I could see the top of the mountain. I was almost out of breath and the muscles in my legs were screaming at me to stop, but with new energy in my step, I walked faster and then broke into a tired run to the top, until finally, I made it. I bent over, hands on my knees, gasping for breath, not bothering to push the hair out of my face.

Then I turned around and realized why I had kept going. In front of me was what is, to this day, one of the most beautiful sights I have ever seen. I was on top of the Rocky Mountains. I looked down the vista and saw the Rockies fading into the distance. Behind me was nothing but wilderness for miles. I had conquered the mountain and now stood on top of the world.

I looked down maybe two or three thousand feet at the road. A car passed by, and I couldn't help feeling sorry for the driver who unwittingly drove past a journey that ended with such triumph and beauty. My eyes drifted to my car in the cutout below. It was no bigger than a speck in my vision, and it quickly put in perspective how far I had actually come. It put in perspective, next to the entirety of the mountain range, what I had conquered and what I had won.

We live in an age that tells us the way to find happiness and success is quickly. We're encouraged to take shortcuts and the easy way, or sometimes to just not bother to take a journey at all.

Hungry? Don't find, cultivate, and prepare ingredients for a beautiful meal. Pull into a drive-through for some fast food.

Overweight? Don't take time and patience to learn how to eat well. Take a pill.

Not strong enough? Don't commit to working out and going through the pain of tearing your muscles over a long period of time. Take steroids.

Sad? Don't worry about processing those ugly emotions. Go abuse substances and drink until the feelings are gone.

Lonely? Don't waste time waiting to meet someone special and put in the effort to cultivate a relationship. Get on a hookup app and get what you want in a couple of hours.

The list goes on and on. And none of us are immune to this kind of thinking. I can't tell you how many times I've wanted to give up on this journey to becoming a good man, to just decide it's a silly notion and give in to what the world tells me is acceptable.

But we see again and again the downside of this kind of thinking. Like the people in the cars passing by as I stood on top of the mountain, we prefer to stay in the comfort of what's easy rather than beginning the journey of what's worthy. The often harsh but beautiful reality of life is that anything worthwhile takes time, dedication, and commitment to a vision. This is true of everything, including running a marathon, learning a language, losing weight, making friends, wooing a woman, or becoming a good man.

Nothing truly good comes easy and nothing easy is truly good. The truly good things in this life don't happen overnight. Rather, they happen night after night after night. We will not immediately accomplish the things we long for, reach the goals we set out to reach, or become the men we want to be.

And this is frustrating. I can't tell you how many times I've looked at myself in the mirror and hated the person looking back at me. I get so frustrated with the slow progress I've made. I find myself dealing with the same weaknesses, falling into the same pitfalls, and fighting the same demons I did ten years ago—and it often makes me want to give up altogether, just like the time I thought about turning back midway through my journey up the mountain. But if I do, if I had, oh, what I would've missed.

As I look at the lives of the men I admire, the men I aspire to be like, I find that none of them got to be all they wanted to be right away or quickly. Instead, their greatness came from slow, steady work and perseverance. Their journey to the mountaintop took years of blood, sweat, and tears. And they only made it to the peak because they knew that the present pain was nothing compared to the future glory.

They didn't give up when it got hard; they pushed even harder.

They didn't stay down when they tripped or were pushed down; they got up.

Being a good man isn't about having it all together right now or reaching a destination quickly. Being a good man is simply committing to the journey of becoming the man you were made to be, no matter how long or hard the road is. It's the choice to take the first step of the journey and then continue on even when you're hurt or feeling weak.

Jesus told a story about the ones who will enter the kingdom of heaven, comparing each of us to seeds. In Mark 4:3–9, He said,

> "Listen! A farmer went out to plant some seed. As he scattered it across his field, some of the seed fell on a footpath, and the birds came and ate it. Other seed fell on shallow soil with underlying rock. The seed sprouted quickly because the soil was shallow. But the plant soon wilted under the hot sun, and since it didn't have deep roots, it died. Other seed fell among thorns that grew up and choked out the tender plants so they produced no grain. Still other seeds fell on fertile soil, and they sprouted, grew, and produced a crop that was thirty, sixty, and even a hundred times as much as had been planted!" Then he said, "Anyone with ears to hear should listen and understand."

We each can find ourselves in this story, but it is up to us what the outcome will be. Will we be the ones who have good intentions but never leave the beaten path, getting eaten up by the pleasures and alluring but temporary thrills of the world? Will we be the ones who look good but plant ourselves in shallow, easy soil that can't sustain the heat and winds of this life? Will we be the ones who plant ourselves around thorns that choke out the life we want? Or will we take the time, effort, and work to plant, till, and root ourselves in soil that will withstand all this broken world has to offer and end up producing life? The choice is ours.

I say all of this as an incomplete and imperfect man who has made mistakes and fallen more times than I could or would like to count. But I have made the choice to take this journey, and I am finding more wisdom, more peace, more triumph, and most of all, a clearer picture of who I was made to be.

Through the struggle, the fight, and the relentless temptation to give up, something deep within me knows I must keep going, that this journey is a worthy and important one. There's something written on my soul, telling me that if I choose to keep following the voice of my Creator, toward the man He made me to be, I will experience the importance of this journey. That this choice will not only impact me now but echo in eternity.

Will you make that commitment and join me on the path to becoming a good man?

Questions for Reflection

1. Have you ever felt like not starting on the path to being a good man? Have you felt like giving up? How have you overcome those thoughts?

2. What can you do to inspire yourself to keep going?

3. Who do you want to be and where do you want to end up? Are you on your way?

> Therefore, since we are surrounded by such a huge crowd of witnesses to the life of faith, let us strip off every weight that slows us down, especially the sin that so easily trips us up. And let us run with endurance the race God has set before us.
>
> Hebrews 12:1

A PRAYER FOR
THE COMMITTED

God, who is as faithful and constant as we are not,
help us to grow every moment, every hour, every
day in the ability to consistently turn our attention
to You. Help us to find new inspiration that will
strengthen our determination to follow You and not
grow weary of the journey You have laid before us.

Let us not be taken with the things that seek only to
lull our minds and hearts. Let us not be distracted
by the alluring but ultimately hollow pleasures
of this world. Let us break our addiction to the
comfort and lethargy that calls to us. Instead, let
us fix our eyes on the prize that lies ahead.

Give us endurance and an awareness of Your
presence as we choose to keep going, keep fighting,
and keep on keeping on, knowing all along it is
Your strength, not ours, that will see us through.

Amen.

Afterword

What Now?

Whenever I come to the end of a book that was written to teach me or reveal truth, often my first reaction is a question.

"What now?"

Stories, concepts, and lessons are great, but sometimes connecting the words on a page to a real world with real questions, problems, and trials can be a daunting task. This question of "What now?" is especially pressing when we are talking about something as big, important, and intimidating as becoming good men, becoming the men we were *made* to be.

So as we come to the end of this book, I want to find a simple but meaningful way to take the things we've talked about, struggled with, and fought to understand and apply them to our daily lives in a realistic and practicable way—a way that helps us take the first steps on this journey of becoming good men.

I've talked a lot about becoming a good man, so it makes sense to me to end this book by talking about the *best* man, Jesus. I truly believe that in the person of Jesus we find the perfect image of a good man. When we are lost, we can simply look at His words and His actions and we will see everything we should be and strive to become.

Not much is written about Jesus in between His being a child and a His being a thirty-year-old man—just one verse, actually, and one we might quickly skip over if we're not careful. I found this verse when I decided I wanted to be a good man, a man after God's own heart. For many years it has led me when I've found myself straying, tiring, and tripping. It's provided guidance in times of confusion and inspiration in times of despair.

Jesus grew in wisdom and in stature and in favor with God and all the people. (Luke 2:52)

It's a short verse, but in it we find four distinct ways Jesus grew, matured, and lived.

Wisdom

Wisdom is mentioned repeatedly in Scripture. In the Old Testament, Solomon was given a choice of anything he wanted, and he asked God for wisdom and was blessed for it. Wisdom is important to God because He knows how necessary it is for us to grow into the men we are supposed to be. In step with Jesus, we can begin every day chasing wisdom and building truth into our souls. We must take the time to read, listen, and engage with the things that will broaden our minds and deepen our understanding of this truth in a world that so often throws out lies. Perhaps that's reading more books, listening to a podcast, or taking a class.

Stature

Stature refers to Jesus's physical growth, as He grew older and went from living in the body of a boy to that of a man. This verse demonstrates that our physical health and growth are important to God. This doesn't mean that to be a good man we must be ripped with six-pack abs (if that were a requirement, I'd be out). But it does mean that taking care of our bodies is a necessary aspect of becoming a whole man. This will look different for all of us. For me, it's learning portion control, not bingeing, eating healthier, getting outside, and sticking to a regular workout routine, even if it's just twenty minutes a few times a week. But for us to live and move at our best in this world, we must take care of the bodies God has given us. Like Jesus, we will grow in stature.

Favor with God

This one perhaps is the most important of all the ways Jesus grew, matured, and lived, for out of it our healing and strength will grow. Jesus devoted time to His relationship with His heavenly Father. We must too. We *must* take the time and effort to grow closer to God and allow Him into our lives, something that is possible only with dedication. I struggle with keeping regular prayer times and reading Scripture. My mind often wanders, and sometimes the craziness of life distracts me. But I feel the need to connect with my Creator. And when I do, I find myself a more centered and whole man.

Finding favor with God is integral to our journey to becoming good men. Without it, we would be lost. Whatever you need to be doing to grow closer to and foster obedience to God, do it! Not out of guilt or fear but out of the truth that you'll become a better, stronger, and more whole man when you follow God.

All the People

Jesus said, "Your love for one another will prove to the world that you are my disciples" (John 13:35). To do this thing right and walk this path well, we need other people. We need to love and to be loved. To know and to be known. To strengthen others and to be strengthened. It is how we were made; humans need one another. So, as a final tenet for practically living a life like Jesus, I dedicate time and energy to building relationships, to knowing and loving others. In return, I find they do the same for me. It's the way God made us and an important piece of becoming a good man. There are many ways to connect with those around us and fully live into being a good man. Maybe that means joining a small group at church or going back to church to begin with. Maybe that means having coffee with someone you can invest in or learn from or inviting a few guys over for a movie night. Whatever it is, remember that we need one another on this path.

———

It is my hope that in each of these categories you can find and create practical ways to move forward on this path of becoming a good man. More than anything, I want you to remember that we are not perfect and never will be, but we were created with a purpose that will change the world and echo into eternity. It won't be an easy journey, and we will fall along the way, but what sets apart a good man is the determination to get up, accept God's grace and love, and with His help, keep trying.

I'm in it with you, and God is in it with us.

Let's do this, men.

Acknowledgments

Thank you to my father, Clay, for all the Boys' Nights Out and theological talks in the car, as well as the money, effort, time, and support you have given me since I was born. Thank you for showing me what a faithful man really looks like.

Thank you to my brother, Joel, for the hours of video games you played with your little brother, acting out The Lord of the Rings, teaching me how to read, tying my shoes, riding bikes, and providing a constant example of an upright man.

Thank you to my mother, Sally, for the read-aloud times from books about heroes, calling me "a man after God's own heart" for as long as I can remember, and every phone call, heart talk, and moment you spent lovingly shaping me into a better man in the midst of my differences.

Thank you to my sisters, Sarah and Joy, for putting up with me and laughing along with all my teasing, jokes, and brotherly love. Thank you for being true pictures of what good women are.

Thank you to Keelia, for fully embracing this out-of-the-box man, softening my hard heart with gentle love, and being my person in the best and hardest moments.

Thank you to my dearest friend, Lou, for prayers in the morning together, pizza and movies on Friday nights, countless talks about God, and a safe place to land and write this book in a big and weary city.

Thank you to my friends Matt, Ben, and Chad, for all the late-night talks in the hot tub about God, road trip adventures with blaring rock music, and allowing me to be a part of a gang for over a decade.

Thank you to my therapist, Jeff, for listening with compassion to the deepest and darkest parts of my soul while giving me a safe place to begin this journey of questioning, redefining, and discovering what a good man really is. And finally, thank you to every man—good and bad, strong and weak—along my path of life who has showed me a clear picture of who I do and do not want to be.

Notes

Chapter 1 Adventurous

1. "Suicide Statistics," American Foundation for Suicide Prevention, accessed October 24, 2019, https://www.nimh.nih.gov/health/statistics /suicide.shtml; Centers for Disease Control and Prevention, "Leading Causes of Death (LCOD) by Age Group, All Males—United States, 2015," April 16, 2018, https://www.cdc.gov/healthequity/lcod/men/2015/all-males /index.htm; Ricky Hatton, "Watch: Our Expert Panel Talks Mental Health," October 24, 2017, https://www.menshealth.com/uk/mental-strength /a758164/watch-our-expert-panel-talks-mental-health/.

2. Megan Hull, "Pornography Facts and Statistics," The Recovery Village, September 12, 2019, https://www.therecoveryvillage.com/process-addiction /porn-addiction/related/pornography-statistics/#gref.

3. "20 Alarming Domestic Violence Statistics for 2018," Social Solutions, accessed October 24, 2019, https://www.socialsolutions.com/blog/domestic -violence-statistics-2018/; Statista Research Department, "Number of Mass Shootings in the United States between 1982 and August 2019, by Shooter's Gender," Statista, September 2, 2019, https://www.statista.com/statistics /476445/mass-shootings-in-the-us-by-shooter-s-gender/; "Gang Statistics," US Department of Justice, accessed October 24, 2019, https://www.justice .gov/jm/criminal-resource-manual-103-gang-statistics; Dr. Scott A. Bonn, "Serial Killer Myth #3: They Are All Men," *Psychology Today*, August 18, 2018, https://www.psychologytoday.com/us/blog/wicked-deeds/201408 /serial-killer-myth-3-they-are-all-men.

Chapter 2 Devout

1. Robert Robinson, "Come, Thou Fount of Every Blessing," 1757.

Chapter 8 Authentic

1. *Rich Mullins Live*, recorded July 19, 1997, at Carpenter's Way Church in Lufkin, Texas, DVD.

2. Jen Christensen, "The Sad Clown: The Deep Emotions Behind Stand-Up Comedy," CNN Health, December 4, 2018, https://www.cnn.com/20 17/03/01/health/sad-clown-standup-comedy-mental-health/index.html.

Chapter 10 Wise

1. Erin Kayata, "Do You Read More Books Per Year Than the Average American?" *Reader's Digest*, accessed November 4, 2019, https://www.rd .com/culture/do-you-read-more-books-than-average-american/.

2. Jimmy Kimmel, "Can You Name a Country?" *Jimmy Kimmel Live*, July 12, 2018, YouTube video, https://www.youtube.com/watch?v=kRh1 zXFKC_o.

About Nathan

Nathan Clarkson is an actor, author, filmmaker, and artist. He is the coauthor of the bestselling book *Different: The Story of an Outside-the-Box Kid and the Mom Who Loved Him* and has acted in numerous popular TV shows and films. Nathan lives between Los Angeles, New York City, and his hometown of Monument, Colorado.

Get to know
NATHAN!

Visit **nathanclarkson.me** to learn more.

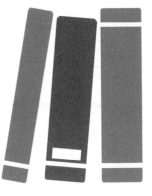

LIKE THIS
BOOK?
Consider sharing it with others!

- Share or mention the book on your social media platforms. Use the hashtag **#GoodMan**.

- Write a book review on your blog or on a retailer site.

- Pick up a copy for friends, family, or anyone who you think would enjoy and be challenged by its message!

- Share this message on Twitter, Facebook, or Instagram: **I loved #GoodMan by @NathanClarkson // @ReadBakerBooks**

- Recommend this book for your church, workplace, book club, or class.

- Follow Baker Books on social media and tell us what you like.

 ReadBakerBooks

 ReadBakerBooks

 ReadBakerBooks